REVIVING
SPIRITUAL
HUNGER

Patrick M. Schatzline

Reviving Spiritual Hunger by Patrick M. Schatzline

Published by
Insight Publishing Group
8801 S. Yale, Suite 410
Tulsa, OK 74137
Phone: (918) 493-1718
Fax: (918) 493-2219

Scripture quotations marked KJV are from
the King James Version of the Bible.

Scripture quotations marked NKJV are from
the New King James Version of the Bible.
Copyright © 1979, 1980, 1982 by Thomas Nelson Inc.,
publishers. Used by permission.

Scripture quotations marked NLT are from the
Holy Bible, New Living Translation, copyright © 1996
by Tyndale House Publishers. Used by permission.

Scripture quotations marked AMP are from the Amplified
Bible. Old Testament copyright © 1965, 1987 by
Zondervan Corporation. The Amplified New Testament
copyright © 1954, 1958, 1987 by the Lockman
Foundation. Used by permission.

Acknowledgments

I want to thank some people, without whom this book would not be possible.

I want to thank my wife, sons and daughter for their support and patience. My wife, Deb, has been a support, an encourager and also an inspiration. I cannot imagine accomplishing anything of significance without her by my side.

I wish to thank DayStar. They are the best church in the world and inspire me every Sunday.

Also my secretaries, especially Karen. Only God knows the patience she has shown as she helped gather, type and edit. She has protected me like a mother hen over her chicks.

Then I want to give special thanks to Deborah Poulalion who has edited, chopped, suggested and compiled beyond belief. She has taught me more than she can ever realize. Only God could have sent her.

Then there are those in ministry who have taught me friendship by experience: John Bevere, John Ritcheson, Anthony, Mickey and Vesta Mangun, Al Brice, Murray Kelly, Frankie Powell, Philip Cameron, Vaudie Lambert, Pat Stone, Neville McDonald, Fred Roberts, Gary Dopson, Ezekiel Guti, Troy and Vicki Hodges, and many others who believed in me when I didn't believe in myself.

But most of all I want to thank Jesus. He came after me when no one else would have. I love Him.

Contents

Foreword

HIRELING, SERVANT OR friend. All who profess Jesus fall into one of these three categories. The question is: which one? We all would like to be considered *His* friend. There is no higher call or greater honor. Yet, is it possible to consider ourselves friends of God while He is of a different opinion? It is God, not us, who names His friends. Jesus admonished, "You are My friends if..." (John 15:14, NKJV). There's a definite condition placed upon His friendship.

The Scriptures clearly warn many will speak of a relationship with Him that just does not exist. How sobering to think of multitudes who will hear Him one day say, "I never knew you!" (Matt. 7:23, NKJV).

The high calling of Christianity is to know Him intimately. We are warned we can cast out demons, work miracles and do other wonders in His name, yet not know Him. Knowing Him is not about what we do for Him. It is the pursuit of Him. This fosters unconditional obedience, fueled by both love and holy fear. God promises, "Friendship with the Lord is reserved for those who fear him" (Ps. 25:14, NLT).

The truth in this stirring and revealing book will shine God's light on you and reveal the true condition of your relationship with Him. Though it may shake you to wake you, I challenge you to read it with an open heart. Embrace the relationship with God for which you were created. I don't believe it is an accident you hold this book.

Pat Schatzline is a personal friend. If I were limited to one description of him it would be "a man who truly loves Jesus." This love drew me to him years ago and continues to be the basis of our friendship. I know he speaks the truth to me, void of flattery or condemnation. He is passionate about truth, righteousness and holiness. These pages reveal not only his heart but also a glimpse of the heart of God.

—JOHN BEVERE
AUTHOR/SPEAKER
John Bevere Ministries
Colorado Springs, Colorado

Preface

ONE WORD DESCRIBES the biggest hindrance to spiritual growth among Christians today—satisfaction. Too many of us think we know God well enough. After all, we've heard (or preached!) hundreds of sermons. We can pray on demand. And we don't commit the gross sins that other people do.

But do we *know* Him? So many are desperate for direction from God because they don't know Him well enough to know what He wants. My goal is to spark within you a hunger to know God that will transform your relationship with Him. The first four chapters of this book focus on increasing spiritual hunger. The rest of the book talks about how spiritual hunger will take you through three levels of relationship with God—hireling, servant and friend.

We all start our relationship with God as hirelings—those who serve God for what He will do for them. It's not wrong to start this way, but too many people stay at this level. They are never challenged to put effort into having a deeper relationship with the Lord. When a church is stuck at this level, it can be very destructive, as I'll describe.

Many believers who are in ministry positions have progressed up to the next level, and they have a servant relationship with the Lord. At this level, they work hard and try to be obedient. When a church is operating at the servant level, it is blessed with unity. At the same time, those at this level must resist temptation toward self-righteousness or martyrdom.

The goal of our relationship with God is to reach a level of friendship and grow into it. I freely admit that I have not arrived at where I should be, but I am working every day to get there. People who have friendship with God will experience the power of the resurrection and be transformed into His likeness, as it says in Philippians 3:10. I am always inspired when I read this passage. (I particularly like the Amplified version.)

> [For my determined purpose is] that I may know Him [that I may progressively become more deeply and intimately acquainted with Him, perceiving and recognizing and understanding the wonders of His Person more strongly and more clearly], and that I may in that same way come to know the power outflowing from His resurrection [which it exerts over believers], and that I may so share His sufferings as to be continually transformed [in spirit into His likeness even] to His death, [in the hope].
>
> —Philippians 3:10, Amp.

I have heard a pithy and quaint quote over and over from various pulpits. It goes something like this; "If you want church-wide revival draw a circle on the ground and get in it. When revival comes to that circle then it will be in the church."

What a great thought, but no one ever stops to give instructions on getting revival into that circle. The thought, however good, is left hanging in air. I pray that the following pages give each reader the steps to filling that circle with spiritual fire.

I am so hungry for God. Do you want to be hungry, too? If you are ready to walk closer to Him than you ever have before, then read on.

Chapter 1

Let's Stop Pretending

How would you describe your relationship with God? Everything in Christianity rises and falls on individual relationship with Him. We are the church. Do you know God? Or do you still wonder what it even means to know God?

For many years I struggled with my need to know God and my seeming inability to even grasp what that meant. King David is a hero to me because of the effort he put into knowing God. He had already seen King Saul's passing and had brought the ark of the covenant back to Jerusalem. He was so filled with the need for relationship that he had the ark placed in an open-sided tent behind the palace rather than returned to the tabernacle of Moses.

Each morning as the sun rose, choirs sang praises. King David exited the back door of the palace and descended the steps.

As the sun rose over the horizon, the rays flashed across the landscape and struck the ark itself. The raised wings of the cherubim on the mercy seat cast a long, distended shadow that reached clear to the bottom of the palace steps.

King David knelt in that shadow and began his morning oblation and praise. As the sun rose, the shadow shortened. The king remained in the ever-shortening shadow by crawling ever closer and closer to the ark.

Finally he would be almost directly under the mercy seat itself.

It was out of this daily exercise that David is said to have quoted Moses, "He that dwelleth in the secret place of the Most High shall abide under the shadow of the Almighty" (Ps. 91:1, KJV).

All this to get close. Still, David's effort seems like very little when you compare it to Jesus coming to earth and dying just to get to know us.

THE CHOIR'S ATTITUDE

I wonder how the singers in David's choir felt. Did they understand what it was all about? It is quite probable that for many of them it was a bother. They had to get up early, the weather was unpredictable, and for some it was just a job. After all, what did all this mean?

Today's church may not be all that different in attitude. It seems that many Christians, that is, church attenders, are confused. Many have little if any understanding about the purpose of church meetings. I'm afraid many think it is a simple matter of fulfilling a God-designated duty—a duty designed by the Almighty to show us who holds our leash.

To still others it is an hour as near to eternal torment as they will ever have to endure. Since they put in fifty-two hours a year, they get to miss hell itself. They hope for bonus points if they drop a little money in the offering. Devoid of joy, there is no real worship and certainly no real relationship. It is as though Jesus went through all He did to form a simple passing acquaintance with His bride the church.

In an unusual, if not ghastly and morbid view of God and His church, attenders act as though every service were a funeral. How remarkable this would be to those of the New Testament church who chose to worship on Sunday in celebration of the resurrection rather than the traditional Saturday, Sabbath.

It seems to be an exclusive attribute of the church not to be able to recognize when a local church is dead. No one visits a funeral home and takes everyone's pulse to see which one is dead. It is obvious! The dead one is not functioning in any of the ways he or she was designed to function. Dead is defined as something that once had life and now has none.

What makes this even more extraordinary is that the Gospels show it was impossible to have a funeral once Jesus arrived. Yet here is an entity filled with people who walk the streets bearing His name. Then they get up in church on Sunday and try to convince each other that He has come to church. From the pulpit someone in authority will ask in a hollow tone, "How many of you know Jesus is here? I brought Him with me, didn't you?"

I can imagine the funeral director of Nain setting a watch at the city gate hoping Jesus doesn't come to town again or he'll miss being paid because of another unfinished funeral. (See Luke 7:11–17.)

Yet today's church doesn't seem to even be able to discern whether or not Jesus has arrived without a show of hands. In many places He wouldn't even pull a majority of the vote.

How absurdly ridiculous! If Jesus shows up something will happen—something inexplicable and totally irrational. Much of what we believe is just that.

- A doctor diagnoses an incurable condition. We rub a little Crisco on the forehead and speak a few words and that person is made perfectly whole.
- A family is in a terrible financial strain. We tell them that if they donate ten percent of what they have to God they will have more.
- A marriage that is teetering on the brink of a painful, child-dividing, squabbling divorce has every anger, fear and betrayal washed away in their tears.
- A drug addict is suddenly set free without withdrawals. All his selfish, self-serving attributes are changed, and now he lives a life of sacrifice and service to others.

None of this is rational. But that doesn't determine its reality.

After all, how much sense does it make to say that a God who has no beginning and no end died for me! It is impossible! But that didn't stop Him from doing it.

EXCUSES CALLED "DOCTRINE"

If we could understand all the ways of God we would

4

be God, instead of Him. He gave us a rule book. It is to be our guide for operation. The whole of Christianity must remain within the boundaries of the Bible.

The problem seems to be that somewhere down the line we stopped following the biblical model. No more miracles.

Instead of stopping and asking ourselves what the problem was, the church came up with excuses for God and called it doctrine. Or, as is the case of many Pentecostal churches, they just went on doing what they always did and pretended it was working. And if by chance a miracle did seem to occur, they acted as though it were blind dogged faith and the repetition of hollow formulas that did it. As quickly as the testimony went forth, the church sitting in the pews had already decided the doctor made an error in diagnosis.

We need a heaven-rending revival. We need prayer and fasting until the divine interruption arrives. But it is only for the hungry.

When Jesus fed five thousand men, they all ate till they were full. The leftovers were not collected till the people had eaten as much as they wanted (John 6:1-14). If it were today's church being fed the bread of life, I'm afraid a lot more than twelve baskets would be left over. The church just isn't hungry.

I personally have never gotten full. I want more of Jesus and less of me! If the rest of the church is full I want God to leave the leftovers for me. I'll be glad to eat them. I haven't as yet had as much as I want. I am sooooo hungry! I figure the leftovers are what gives us the strength to stand in the face of the world's hell.

Our sleepy, sedate, malnourished church must stir itself to eat!

Chapter 2

Learning to Be Hungry

SEVERAL PEOPLE HAVE asked me lately what I mean by the term "spiritual hunger." This question always stuns me. But I am told that children who are dying of malnutrition lose their ability to feel hunger. They must be forced to eat meals until their bodies are reacquainted with the difference between being full or hungry. Many Christians are so malnourished they need to be taught to hunger and thirst for more of Jesus.

I have learned what Paul found at Ephesus when he asked about the infilling of the Holy Spirit. They responded, "We have not so much as heard of the Holy Spirit" (Acts 19:2).

Many have no idea whatsoever that there is more of Jesus to be had. In this chapter I'll refute the idea that it can be dangerous to seek after God; I'll describe pure spiritual hunger; and I'll tell how to resist intimidation from others that would quench your hunger.

Some have been taught that you can get yourself into deep spiritual trouble seeking for more of Jesus in your life. As absurd as this sounds it is still preached in many circles. This, of course, is easily dispelled by reading Jesus' instructions to His disciples in Matthew 7:6–11.

> Ask, and it shall be given you; seek, and ye shall find; knock, and it shall be opened unto you: For every one that asketh receiveth; and he that seeketh findeth; and to him that knocketh it shall be opened. Or what man is there of you, whom if his son ask bread, will he give him a stone? Or if he ask a fish, will he give him a serpent? If ye then, being evil, know how to give good gifts unto your children, how much more shall your Father which is in heaven give good things to them that ask him? (KJV).

In fact, if it is possible to seek Jesus and receive anything satanic, then what in the world are we doing praying to the weaker of the two! Somewhere along the line I must be confident that my Lord is capable of protecting me. It is the demonic that must back off! "Greater is He that is in you" (1 John 4:4, KJV). I certainly don't mean to be insensitive to other's views, but that theological perspective is about as dumb as dirt. Some folks just need to lay their intellect aside and get a relationship with Jesus. If they do, it won't be long before He reveals to them how truly big and powerful He is.

There is absolutely no scriptural basis for teaching that the demonic power of hell can take over when you're praying to God. This is a theological concept formed in the minds of men who felt they needed to explain some ugly situations to God.

I admit that some bad situations can arise when a person who is already unbalanced mentally and/or emotionally seeks God to fill an abnormal void in his life. He is operating with the wrong motivation. In operating in the wrong or in an emotionally confused agenda anything can happen. But the person who is truly hungry for Jesus out of a spiritual hunger, without other agendas, will be fully protected. The question isn't whether you are big and powerful enough spiritually to touch Him. It is whether He is big enough to speak and protect us.

I can understand that a person can want something so badly that the motive loses its purity without losing its sincerity. But you cannot twist God's arm to get what you want. I have at times seen some with such a lust for ministry that their agenda is as twisted as it is impure. They so desperately want to hear a voice that tells them what they are already thinking that Satan will give them one. But when a heart is yielded and open, loving and hungry for God just as He is, I don't believe for an instant that anything demonic can take over.

SELF-RIGHTEOUSNESS IS THE TRAP

I pastor a wonderful church that is perpetually hungry. If there is any danger from spiritual hunger, it comes from man's tendency toward self-righteousness. For example, there is someone praying in my church sanctuary twenty-four hours a day. Individuals sign up for three-hour prayer watches. There is suitable music playing in the sanctuary at all times, and each prayer shift will have at least one and as many as fifteen praying at any given time.

Jesus has met us and blessed us marvelously as a result of prayer. But after several years of full-time prayer seven days a week, a strange edge come into the church. As I sought God concerning this the Holy Spirit was quick to reveal self-righteousness. To my embarrassment, it was creeping into the church from pastor to pew. I asked the Holy Spirit what we must do and He said to go to six days a week for prayer and leave Sunday as a day to receive, so we would understand that it wasn't by might or power but by His Spirit.

It is so easy to think that good things are happening at my church because of our works or physical faithfulness. We are so blessed! For five years in a row at our annual church business meeting we had at least five saved and as many as eight filled with the Holy Spirit after the devotion. At a business meeting! When that happens, everyone has to know that it is God and God alone.

There were several reasons we shouldn't have gotten self-righteous:

1. The idea for this kind of prayer wasn't original with me. There is a Pentecostal church in Alexandria, Louisiana, that has been doing this for decades. Needless to say they have had an incredible impact on their city for Christ. I still visit there for pure refreshing. Just sitting in that church I sense an awesome anointing that has saturated the place.

2. There are many good churches in the world and even in our own city. It is unacceptable for any church to think they are so on the agenda of Jesus that everyone else must catch up.
3. I as a leader should have known better. I should have recognized it in myself before it ever was passed to the congregation. After all, you reproduce what you are. Cows do not birth kangaroos.

I am so thankful I serve a merciful God. And now Sunday is our day to gratefully receive from Him who is All in All. This has filtered our motivation and purified it. We do not pray to become anything but His.

We are not better or worse than any other church. The purpose of the cross was to bring sinful man into relationship with a holy God. Any church fulfilling this purpose is anointed or it wouldn't be happening.

We must give ourselves to the search for a deeper more intimate relationship with Jesus. This will always benefit both the individual and the kingdom. God's will and purpose will be performed.

THE GOAL OF SPIRITUAL HUNGER

The goal of spiritual hunger is to become so close to Jesus that we meld with Him in spirit. His every whisper becomes a command to which we find ourselves radically obedient. It is to live a biblical lifestyle filled with holiness, reverence and godly awe. Whatever Jesus wishes to do in any given situation we find ourselves doing. We simply are constantly available to Him.

The Christian, then, is on a journey to become so transparent and focused in life that everyone who looks at us sees Jesus larger than they saw Him before. Our lives simply magnify Him. This isn't a new concept. Charles Sheldon wrote of a church operating in this philosophy in his classic book *In His Steps*.

It is drawing so close to Jesus in your relationship that somehow the shadow of Jesus mixes with yours. I'm not completely sure how to get there as yet, but that it can be done is a certainty. Simon Peter did, and that gives me a scriptural precedent to stand on.

> And believers were the more added to the Lord, multitudes both of men and women. Insomuch that they brought forth the sick into the streets, and laid them on beds and couches, that at the least the shadow of Peter passing by might overshadow some of them.
> —ACTS 5:14–15, KJV

This lifestyle will express itself as much by what is missing as by what is there. It will lack envy and jealousy of other ministries. It will be seen by its ability to rejoice in the accomplishments of other saints. There will be satisfaction when others are blessed even when it appears as though the things you touch are far from blessed.

OBEY THE WORD, NOT MAN

I am convinced that many God-fearing, Bible-believing saints have never been confronted with others who are hungry. They love and serve God with all of their hearts, but no one told them they couldn't be sport-aholics, workaholics or knowledge-aholics. They just think Jesus is to be fitted into their already overcrowded schedules. They can shout at ballgames, spend long hours at work, have an unquenchable hunger for earthly knowledge and even knowledge about God but never desire to know Him better. They have never been told that there should be a deep desire to know Him. In fact, that is their definition for a fanatic.

Don't get me wrong. They are often well-meaning folks. Often they are simply quoting someone who is or was their spiritual authority. To admit there may be more feels very nearly like some form of spiritual betrayal to that past or present leader. And no one wants to betray the spiritual leaders who love them. But it isn't betrayal at all.

If you are going to give God your whole heart, that very surrender must include surrender to a higher authority. This higher authority is the Word of God. Read the Bible. These things are not hidden from those in love with Jesus. Psalm 138:2 states that God has exalted His Word above His name.

The Word of God tells us what should and should not happen when we come together to worship. People will ask why we do what we do in church. We must have a better answer than "that it is our tradition." The Lord said in Colossians 2:8:

> Beware lest any man spoil you through phi-losophy and vain deceit, after the tradition of men, after the rudiments of the world, and not after Christ (KJV).

We must have a scriptural reason. Every worship

service must give God what He asks for and what pleases Him.

Somewhere, sometime, someone first was so amazed at God he lifted his hands and God saw it. He looked over at the angels in glee and said, "Put that in the Book. I like it." Another time somewhere someone got so excited she started shouting out loud and praising God, and God so enjoyed it He said, "Put that in My Book." Then sometime later, somewhere someone started clapping his hands when he shouted and God said, "I really like that! Put that in the Book."

Then when something extremely enjoyable and blessed happened to another person she began to jump up and spin wildly and dance. God said, "That is very, very good. Put it in My Book." You see, we should be doing what pleases and blesses God when we come together, not what feels comfortable and seems to be socially acceptable. Read the Book. True worship has never been socially acceptable. The religious will never tolerate what God prescribes to be done. But how can we possibly begin to accept any other standard of conduct than the one God Himself authored? His Word and the Christ it contains is what sets us apart from every other religion in the world.

I have never understood the Christian church operating on any other authority. Our style of worship and service has been for the most part a socially acceptable, worldly controlled environment. It is time we humbled ourselves and accepted correction. We must stop allowing the world to intimidate us into worship services that largely resemble funerals.

RESIST INTIMIDATION

Intimidation is a satanic strategy to make us disobey God's Word and lose our spiritual hunger. We need men and women of God who will stand up to those who have fallen to intimidation. And if we are the ones being corrected, we need to heed God's warning. See how this occurs when Paul confronted Peter at Antioch. Here's the scene.

Simon Peter and Barnabas are visiting the church at Antioch. This is Simon Peter, the man who had received the vision on the rooftop that had sent him to preach the gospel at a gentile's house (Acts 10). Now at Antioch he has been intimidated by the other Jewish Christians. It seems that while he was sitting and supping with the non-Jewish believers the Jews had begun teasing and berating him surreptitiously. It so bothered him that he not only stopped eating with the Gentiles but had also persuaded Barnabas to do likewise (Gal. 2:11–21).

When Paul arrives he is absolutely stunned by what he sees. Paul hated prejudice! That was just one of the many ugly things God had delivered him from.

Without a moment's hesitation, Paul confronts Simon Peter. In today's vernacular, he got in Paul's face. (See Galatians 2:11.) In fact it is even stronger than that in the Greek. It is *anthistemi*, "to stand against and oppose to the face." It simply states that Paul left no room for possible misinterpretation of his intentions to correct Simon of wrongdoing. He was bold and sharp to the point of being slightly physical.

I can just imagine Paul walking away, shaking his head and mumbling under his breath as he goes, leaving behind a stunned, red-faced and silent Simon Peter.

And then a Judaizer next to Simon Peter elbows him and says in outrage:

Simon! Does he know who he is talking to? Why, you're one of the original twelve. Jesus Himself chose you. You walked and talked, ate and slept with the Lord personally for three-and-a-half years. It was you who had the very first revelation that Jesus was the Christ. Simon, does he know you walked on water? Tell him, Simon, what it was like on the Mount of Transfiguration. You were the first to preach at Pentecost and had three thousand respond to the altar call. I'll bet he hasn't had three thousand saved in his whole ministry.

Why, Simon, people have been healed just by getting in your shadow. You raised Dorcas from the dead. It was you and John that God used to heal the man at the Gate Beautiful.

Paul has let his role in this go to his head, brother. I mean, after all, has Jesus ever fixed him breakfast on the beach? He has gotten beside himself to talk to you in such a tone. It is plain to me that Paul has become some kind of self-righteous fanatic. Somebody needs to take him down a notch or two for his own good.

But don't you worry about it Simon, my friend, some of us will take care of it. Don't give it a second thought. He just didn't realize who he was talking to.

I can picture Simon Peter sitting there, not uttering a word. The more the man talks, the lower Simon's head hangs. The incident has suddenly robbed him of his appetite. Fish and bread don't seem very palatable right now. Tears trickle down his cheeks as with a trembling voice he responds:

My friend, I'm afraid it is you who doesn't know

who he is talking to. Yes, I was with the Master three-and-a-half years during His ministry here on earth. That is true. But you see, while I was serving, I was also arguing with the others over who was the greatest. I did recognize Him as the Christ, but moments later He was calling me Satan. And I'll tell you now, when God calls you the devil it's on pretty good authority. You can mark it down you're being pretty devilish.

I walked on water (that is true) but when I got my eyes off Jesus I began to sink. It was only His mercy that kept me from drowning. Yes, I preached at Pentecost. But I leapt at the chance to explain the confusion. I didn't want everyone else to be as confused as I had been on the night they came after Jesus in the garden.

I had bragged that I would be willing to die for Him, so when they came after Him I leapt at the chance to prove it and cut a man's ear off. Jesus was disappointed in me and rebuked me. I was so confused that I followed after the soldiers and Jesus, but when I was asked if I were His friend, I said no. Three times!

Do you understand? I said I never knew Him! To top it all off, Jesus himself had warned me this would happen, but I was so full of myself I didn't believe Him till I did it.

You don't at all know who I am. Yes, Jesus fixed me breakfast, but it was His inexhaustible mercy reaching to me after I had failed Him miserably.

My friend, anything and everything I have done that is of any value is due to Him. I have come to the conclusion that I'm just no stinking good without Jesus. I can't even catch fish anymore without His help.

If Jesus is able to operate through me at all it's

because I insist on being teachable. I will accept correction, whether it be from Paul or even you, for that matter. I'd rather be right with Jesus than look good.

Don't worry about it. Let it go, my friend. Paul was right.

May we all accept God's correction as Simon Peter did. Our hunger for God must exceed our desire to look good to others.

Chapter 3

Overcoming Insecurity

RECENTLY I READ that the Hubbell telescope revealed that the universe is still expanding. It says that on the outer edges, stars are still popping into existence. We shouldn't be surprised, after all, when God said, "Let it be," He never told it to stop, and without God Himself telling it to stop it hasn't got the power to do so or even the right to feel complete. God designed the universe to grow.

Everything but man himself was created by simply using His word. He said, "Let it be," and it could not refuse to be nor was there any power able to stop it from being.

Every creature of the earth does exactly as it was created to do. Every planet continues its orbit. Each sun burns. The only time the nature of things is ever disturbed is when the prophet of God speaks under the anointing and then it obeys whether it's the sun standing still or the rain holding off for three-and-a-half years.

There isn't anything in creation besides man that argues with God as to whether it should grow or not. Nor about the role they are to play in creation. Only man is given a choice. Only man can be disobedient to his created nature as well as to his Creator (Rom. 1).

I want more of Jesus because I want to follow God's role for me in creation. I know where I came from. Nothing in life worked for me so long as I was attempting to do it in my own strength. Over twenty years ago now, I was a drug addict and pusher in Detroit, Michigan. Then I heard about a Savior. I have made up my mind to never look back. In fact, I ripped reverse out during my first week of salvation.

Every morning of my life the alarm on my wrist-watch goes off at 9:00 A.M. It isn't set so that I can know if my staff is late for work. It is set to remind me of something more important. Each morning when it goes off I ask myself, "Pat, do you have more of Jesus today than you had yesterday?" Let me assure you I and I alone know the true answer to that question. I have made up my mind that the answer will always be YES! I will have more.

This book is about hungering for more of God and growing beyond where we began as new Christians. As you'll see we often don't realize that there are higher levels to be reached. We are saved and self-satisfied, but we are missing out on so much! In the rest of this chapter I'll tell you how God got my attention and showed me that I needed to work on my relationship with Him—not my reputation as seen through the eyes of others.

MY DAY OF CONFRONTATION

Several years ago I attended a conference sponsored by David Wilkerson titled *A Repentance Gathering.* It was an amazing, life-changing event for me. In the very first service with more than a thousand in attendance, men began to cry out over their sin of wasted years without purpose. We were later told that after the service one or more preachers confessed directly to Brother Wilkerson concerning being in adult video clubs. Great conviction and presence were present.

I sat in the middle of this outpouring numb. Preachers were actually falling on their faces on the floor, but I felt nothing. In the middle of this incredible outpouring I was totally untouched. I felt as if God wanted to deal with me about something, but it was impossible for me to tell for sure.

At the time I was pastoring in a suburb of Birmingham, Alabama. I had left a full-time church that was doing so well we had to set up extra chairs at times because of the size of the crowd.

On the other hand, the new church had just gone through a split along with various other problems. I would rather not define them all in print. They had a new building that would seat approximately four hundred and fifty. The night they voted on me they had eighteen in attendance, counting children and babies.

The church had three sections of pews. That night all the attending adults sat in the front middle pew. My wife and I looked out over a totally empty church, except for one pew.

They couldn't pay me anything and there was no parsonage. With some help from one of the men in the church, my wife and I took what small savings we had and put up walls in the abandoned building where the church services used to be held.

Our makeshift home was located on the side of the hill that the new church building capped. In places you could see the outside through cracks along the windows, and when it rained we often would end up with an inch of water throughout the building. Large slugs would be deposited on the threadbare carpet. We shared our place with lots of critters. The roaches and water bugs were the largest I have ever seen. The first fall we killed over sixty field mice in one month.

One night I was chasing a mouse across the bedroom, and it leapt into an open wall plug and was electrocuted. My wife shouted that even the mice would rather commit suicide than live there.

The church had no money to give us. They were falling behind on payments on all their bills. In fact, it was two and a half years before I got my first paycheck.

My wife and I had taken jobs at minimum wage at a local florist. She was doing arrangements and I was driving the delivery truck, along with a few other duties.

We got paid every two weeks. The week before I went to Wilkerson's conference we had taken both our checks and paid the electric bill of the church. After paying the bill we had one dollar left and no groceries. Yet we both felt the Lord speak to our hearts that we weren't to tell anyone. We both prayed for nearly three days until someone brought us a car trunk load of groceries of all kinds. It was a timed miracle.

Since I was obviously doing God a big favor, I was feeling pretty good about myself. After all, how many pastors would do such a thing? I know you might think I was a little self-righteous. Actually, I was a lot self-righteous. Everything I do for God I try to do well. In this state of mind it was really hard for even an omnipotent God to break through and convict me.

After the service my friend Stan, who was my benefactor in getting me to the meeting, stuck around to ask Brother David a question. I leaned against a wall about forty feet away and waited patiently.

Brother David finished speaking to Stan and then turned toward me and said, "Hey, you."

I immediately looked to see who was behind me, but the room was empty besides me and the two of them. Being a man of spiritual sensitivity and insight I immediately told God I was sorry and repented for anything in me that I might not be aware was there. In fact, I said, "Jesus, if there is anything in me I don't know about, please tell me before You tell him. I'll make it right before he gets over here." But, alas, it doesn't work that way.

Brother Wilkerson came toward me with purpose in his steps and fire in his eyes. As he drew close he began to speak, pointing his finger at my chest. He said, "The Lord says you have been living entirely on your emotions rather than the Spirit and voice of God, and He says He's tired of it. So straighten up. He has plenty of men He could use to do what you're doing."

Boy, did he make me mad. All the pressed down and subdued Detroit rose to a slow boil because, of course, he was exactly right. I felt as if I had been hit across the chest with the two-by-four that I had hidden in my eye.

It was a major turning point in my life. It was as crucial a point as my initial salvation encounter. I was so convicted I could barely breathe.

I didn't say anything. Brother Wilkerson just turned and walked out the side door.

WHAT DID GOD MEAN?

I went to my hotel room about a block away. I was very tired. We had driven for nine hours straight, arriving just in time to check in the hotel and go straight to the service.

But when I laid down, sleep was the farthest thing from me. My mind was going a mile a minute. After about twenty minutes I got dressed and headed back to the conference center.

It had been announced that a room had been set aside as a prayer room. When I arrived it was nearly empty. I desperately needed time alone with God anyway, so solitude was a relief.

I spent all night praying—talking a lot and listening very little. I repented, apologized, defended and at some points tried to vindicate myself. And, of course, God didn't respond to any of it. Peace was unavailable.

Peace had always been difficult for me anyway. I heard sermons explaining how Jesus died so that each of us could have peace. But truthfully, I had never met anyone who had it. Sure, all of us had experienced moments of peace when God's presence was real. And there were times when we knew God wasn't upset with us. But the peace I sought was more than a few moments without divine displeasure. In this prayer room, peace by any definition was evading me, much less a type that passed understanding.

I finally interrupted my monologue at God long enough to attend the morning service. Then, since I was flat broke anyway, rather than go to lunch, I returned to the prayer room. I'm not sure how long I was there. Some people were leaving for the evening service.

I got on my face on the floor. After some time of desperate prayers to what seemed to be a distant God, my prayers began to change. The presence of God descended on me and my whole body began to shake. I was vibrating so profusely that I actually bounced on the floor.

I was told later that someone in the room thought I might be having a seizure. They came over to check on me, and the moment they touched me they fell out in the Holy Ghost.

I was now in a new place in prayer. Everything I was uttering was issuing from a place deep in my inner man. At some point God spoke to me clearly. He asked me three questions.

The first question was, "Pat, would you go witnessing with First Baptist Church next Friday night?"

I was quick to respond. "Yes, Lord, of course I will. I love to witness and tell people about Jesus."

There was a long pause. Then Jesus said, "No you wouldn't, Pat. If they called you and asked you to teach them how, then you would. But if they just put an ad in the paper inviting anyone who wanted to go with them, you wouldn't go. They're Baptist, Pat. You are Assembly of God."

I was heartbroken. It was true. He did know me better than I obviously knew myself. I had a mindset for my own denomination. After all, we had the whole truth. I was very sectarian and foolish. If we had the truth it was suddenly very obvious that the truth didn't have me. Somehow I failed to grasp the knowledge that Truth had become a man.

There was another pause. And then God asked me another question. "Pat, why do you read My Word?"

My reply was immediate. "Lord, I love Your Word. I love the stories of faith and miracles. There is power in every lesson I learn from it. It brings light to my brain."

After another long pause the Lord replied, "No, Pat. You read My Word because you need answers and sermons. You love finding little nuances others have not seen, not because they bring revelation of Me but because they make you feel secure that you have an edge on the competition. Pat, why don't you want to know *Me?*"

I suddenly felt very ashamed and humiliated. I had never considered that He would know the insecurity hidden away deep in my heart. To that point I had spent my whole life attempting to be accepted. At times I had gone to great extremes, which often resulted in terrible bouts of depression when I realized I had only succeeded in looking like a fool.

In fact, my quest for acceptance had been my Achilles' heel while pastoring. Whenever I had to stand against others who seemed more successful than I did, even if I knew I was doing what was right, I would be in the pits of depression for days, if not weeks. In fact, if I wasn't careful, if things got really out of control I was prone to temper tantrums at home. These had become much less house shaking in recent months, but it was only because I bottled the frustration up inside. I desperately needed peace.

Only Jesus could have reached me so smoothly and gently. I wept and wept as the reality that God knew me took hold.

Jesus knew me, but obviously I didn't know Him. I

realized it was time for a change. I had to get real. I'm not sure how long I continued in weeping and repentance, but it was long enough for me to begin to change. I felt change drop inside. I was becoming someone different, someone better, someone without disguise. I believe the real Pat was beginning to appear.

God was attempting a true revelation, not just revelation of Him but also revelation to me of myself. Somehow the knowledge had eluded me that God would want the real me—not the pastor, not the leader, just a man named Pat. With this revelation came new understanding. Peace wasn't a characteristic. It was a place that was found in Him.

There had been another long pause in the conversation. I believe it was an act of mercy on God's part. It gave me a chance to process what was happening. Then the Lord asked me a third question. "Pat, why do you pray?"

By the time Jesus asked me this question, I had grasped the fact that He already knew the answer far better than I. I said, "Lord, I have no earthly idea why I pray. It is totally beyond my comprehension. Why don't You tell me?"

This time the Lord responded with a gentleness that nearly broke my heart. He said, "Pat, you pray because you need things. You need My provision for your family. You need Me to work out problems in your church. You need Me to touch your people. Pat, why don't you want to know Me?"

This interview with Jesus changed my life. It changed my perception of ministry. It drastically changed my prayer life and Bible study. In fact, my life as a whole has never been the same.

This confrontation with God and myself gave me a

new hunger. I am finding the inexpressible joy of knowing Him. No wonder the apostle Paul wrote to those at Philippi that everything else in life is dung in comparison.

There was some immediate change, but most of it has been very gradual. That's how God likes to work on a man. It seems that He really loves the creative process.

I am a new creation (2 Cor. 5:17). The Greek verbiage literally means "I have become, am, and am becoming a new creation."

The angels of God are rejoicing again (Luke 15:10) as Jesus works on me. I pray I never stop learning and that I never stop changing. I like the fact that Jesus loves me just as I am but loves me too much to leave me that way.

RECRUITED WITH A PURPOSE

Paul writes in Ephesians that I have been literally recruited for a purpose (1:5–6). This was no divine whim. I am no longer my own. I belong to Jesus. I am His property. To operate in His will and kingdom I must now operate with His agenda. My motive is His will performed. So success can only be defined by obedience, not even by results. You can actually be a leader with worldwide recognition and financial prosperity but a complete failure by this criteria.

What is a man's value? What, in fact, would be the criteria to be a success? What scale is the kingdom to operate on? If our spirituality can be gauged in crowds, dollar signs or buildings, then why did Jesus give His life?

I personally believe He gave Himself as Creator so

that He could never be outbid by larger crowds, offerings or buildings.

Because God recreated us differently, He desires His church to choose to operate differently. I can't believe that Jesus is pleased with His children who jockey for prestige, titles and positions. He certainly didn't seem to like it when the disciples argued over who was the greatest.

The major problem with each of us struggling to appear successful by the world's standards is that everyone else becomes our opposition. Even those inside the kingdom can be considered our adversaries. I believe Satan has enjoyed many vacation days while pastors, church leaders and various individual saints have picked up his work load of accusation, each one engulfed in a quagmire of low self-esteem, defending their work and life from every other, desperately attempting to out perform one another. It's a rat race of dynamic proportions, with the wounded and dying littering every city.

Before Jesus saved me I was a drug dealer in Detroit. I can't believe how the Christian community jockeys for position just like the drug dealers in my old life. Christianity at this level is every bit as violent and deadly as life was on the street. This mentality has to stop.

In the next chapter I'm going to describe what goes on in a church that is not hungering to know God. I hope it won't remind you of any churches you have attended, but it probably will. The chapter ends with good news, however, because there is a way for the church to repent.

Chapter 4

The Church's New Appetite

MANY CHURCHES HAVE stopped hungering for God and started focusing on looking successful to other Christians instead. But no matter how successful you may appear to be you will never find peace in success. I know pastors who seem to have everything going for them, and yet their emptiness is almost tangible. The rest promised in Hebrews 4:1 evades their grasp. It is as though everything Jesus died to provide is beyond their grasp.

Satan's main job in the church is to keep us from receiving those things Jesus suffered to provide for us. He weaves a web of delusion for all those who make success their standard of acceptance with God. Even those in small churches often succumb to it.

There are whole churches that never see anyone saved, yet they are convinced they are God's bastion of faith in that city. They spend countless hours trying to keep the saved saved. Everything in the church is designed for the comfort of those already there. If anyone else wants in they must shoehorn their way into the clique that controls the place or continue to attend as outsiders.

These churches don't mind visitors. In fact, there is a great deal of talk about them. They feel they have been extremely benevolent in letting a visitor come at all.

Their Christianity is a list of things they no longer do. It becomes part of their spiritual duty to see that no one in that church does anything they don't. The result is a hard-core, disciplined, critical, unfriendly group that is holding the fort for God.

In fact, if anyone does manage to stumble in and get saved they are watched with a critical eye. Everyone nods knowingly and benevolently if they stand to testify. After all, the mature know that if they stand back and watch, the new converts will cool off after awhile. It is almost as though new Christians have to backslide to get along with the rest of the church.

When these congregations hear phrases like "zeal for Your house has eaten Me up" (John 2:17, NKJV), they believe it is speaking only of the cross. Everyone knows we have too much to do in life in order to just survive for us to spend much energy on the pursuit of the lost. I mean, if they want what we've got, let them come after it like everyone else. They had better get what they need from the preaching. After all, that's how the rest of the church achieved their mundane perfection.

Satan's strategy has been most effective. Today's church thinks it is too difficult to pray effectual prayers so they don't even bother trying. Most seem to think we can't win the lost and there is little hope for the backslidden. Worship has been reduced to group singing and an offering. Our churches are designed for every comfort. It doesn't matter whether it's too hot for that young couple visiting, just so old Sister Sarah is warm.

The church hates change. The Bible says, "Sing unto the Lord a new song" (Ps. 149:1, KJV). But we want the old stuff that we can sing while mentally changing the oil in our car or planning next week's shopping list.

If you introduce change or challenge it's the only time voices are lifted above a whisper. Discipleship is out of the question. Why attempt to grow when you have already arrived?

Members speak in tones hollow with false humility as they talk of their little struggling church. It is an abomination to God for people to be given more and more Bible knowledge but never be required to put it into operation.

THE BIBLE CURE: PREACHING AND WORSHIP

But there is a cure for this slow-motion drift into obscurity. It is found by following the Word in preaching and worship.

We need strong, anointed, prophetic, confrontational preaching. Just take a good look at the book of Acts. Paul preached long and hard. He preached until people dozed off and fell out of windows (Acts 20:7–12). When Paul and Silas preached at the temple in Thessalonica, the disgruntled Jews cried out to the city's rulers, "These that have turned the world upside down have come here also" (Acts 17:6, KJV).

Two men are accused of turning the world upside

down. Today's church thinks they are being used powerfully if they can persuade the local Little League baseball team not to schedule games on Wednesday nights. I believe the apostles would weep in disbelief if they saw our anemic prayer meetings and non-biblical style of worship.

We need to return to biblical worship, which is worshipping God the way He wishes, not doing what we want. Sometimes someone will say that they don't clap their hands, dance or shout because it isn't their personality. There are some things in life you cannot change or control, but we choose our attitudes. The same people who are dead quiet in church often are just the opposite when at a ball game or when angry.

They would even be very different if need be at work. But then maybe that company pays better than Jesus. It is simply a question of motivation, not personality. If I told someone I would give them a brand-new Mercedes if they danced a little jig, there isn't a person in this country or probably the world who wouldn't do it.

The Word of God isn't suggestions. It is commands. God decides what He wishes and requires from His creation, and then to make it easy on us He puts it in a book. We need to thank Him for making it understandable, not complain and modify what has been already declared by the immutable purpose of a thrice holy God. We, on the other hand, want to worship in a way that's comfortable, neat and nice for us. We have forgotten who is in charge.

Malachi states that there is a book being kept in heaven of those who fear the Lord and honor His name.

> Then those who feared the Lord spoke to
> one another, and the Lord listened and
> heard them; so a book of remembrance was
> written before Him for those who fear the
> Lord and who meditate on His name.
> —MALACHI 3:16, NKJV

The book of remembrance is in addition to the
book of life. God is moved by worship.

THE CHURCH AWAKENS

I believe the church is finally awakening to its own
lack of power. Satan's devices are becoming more
obvious and less accepted. I sense a new hunger for
intimate relationship with God.

Most of us are familiar with the story of Jacob dis-
guising himself as his brother Esau in order to receive
the spiritual blessing of their father Isaac (Gen. 27). I
have heard many sermons on the incident and its spiritual significance, but there is one aspect I've never
heard anyone mention.

At the time of Jacob's deception, Esau had already
forfeited his claim for the firstborn spiritual heritage.
He sold that birthright to Jacob for a bowl of lentil
soup. The Scripture literally states that he despised or
held as contemptuous the spiritual promises and blessings that would come from his father (Gen. 25:34). He
still would receive some things as the grandson of
Abraham, but he was much more in touch with physical reality than spiritual possibilities.

Esau had everything a young prince could want. He
had several wives, along with much in the way of possessions. He had more than enough servants even for a

lifetime. Although he sold his spiritual birthright he would still inherit the lion's share of his father's estate as the eldest.

But suddenly he seemed very alarmed when he discovered what his brother had done. I don't believe it was greed. He had so much already. Something else was taking place.

Upon finding out his brother received the blessing, he cried out. This gut-wrenching cry carried more than the disappointment of being bested at sibling rivalry. It was deeper and stronger than simple jealousy.

Esau was now over forty years old. It had become very clear to him that wives, servants and possessions were not enough to fill the emptiness of the soul. Pleasure is seasonal. It all passes. Even the life of a successful young sultan leaves one empty when it is bereft of God's touch.

It suddenly hit home with the impact of a locomotive. The terrible longing of his soul may haunt his eternal existence. He cried the cry of the truly desperate. "Surely, Father, there must be some portion of spiritual blessing left for me!"

He must have some tidbit of peace. Some glimmer of hope. A thread that will connect him to YHWH. And Isaac, seeing the desperation, finds a positive, if not powerful, blessing to pass to this child.

It is God's desire that His church get just as soul sick. We have all the accouterments of success without the touch of His blessing. We have learned to look good and sound great, but we are still less than what was promised.

God is stirring. Our hunger is increasing. We long for that presence and power that makes church unexplainable. I believe we are about to be brought to order. God intends for His church to startle the world. It may, in fact, startle itself.

RISKING IT ALL TO TOUCH HIM

The Gospels tell the story of a woman who was so hungry for Jesus that she broke the law just to touch Him. (See Matthew 9, Mark 5, Luke 8.) Let's look at the situation from the woman's point of view. She has lost her strength. The life has been slowly leaving her for twelve long years. Yet her physical suffering is overshadowed by the emotional and social suffering that goes with it.

According to her culture she is unclean. The law demands she be totally ostracized. She cannot go to the synagogue or live with her family. No one is allowed to touch her. Her condition is considered to be punishment by God for a horrendous secret sin.

She now lives in a lean-to shack. She has no one to feed her or fend for her. She has not been hugged by a family member in twelve long years. In all likelihood her family has spent every cent they could spare on her medical treatment without any result. Now she is penniless and alone.

Every week a priest comes by to check for proof that her problem has been remedied. When he sees that she is still unclean he goes to the middle of the street, points at her and cries "unclean" at the top of his voice three times.

This would be equivalent to your pastor getting a confirmed report of your having spoken gossip about another church member. He goes to your house, stands in the middle of the street, points at you and loudly cries "gossip" three times.

Or maybe your pastor discovers that you haven't been paying your tithes for whatever reason, and he stands in the street and cries "thief" three times at the top of his lungs.

Can you imagine the embarrassment and chagrin on a warm, sunny spring day when all the neighbors are in their yards? The big difference between you and the woman, however, is that the woman is being punished for a sin she did not commit. To make it even worse, according to the laws this suffering woman has to cry out "unclean" whenever she is in public so that no one accidentally touches her and has to go through purification. She is untouchable.

Just as the woman is bereft of companionship, the church is bereft of the presence of God. The woman is desperate. She has tried everything and nothing helps. We, the present-hour church, have done everything. We have had glamour and glitz, large crowds, professional music and incredible edifices. But it's the presence we lack. It is as though we haven't been hugged in many years.

Christians are the ones who made me hungry for the presence. They told me when I was drug addict that there was something powerful and supernatural. They told me that when I prayed and worshipped He would come to me.

Just as the woman longs for human touch and companionship, I long for the touch and companionship of the divine. Who can help us?

Then one day she hears that a visitor is coming to town. A man named Jesus. She has heard of His healing and most of all she has heard of His *touch*.

I can picture her as she places herself strategically just out of sight, waiting in a shadow, hoping and praying today is her day. She waits patiently, deter-minedly. Finally there is a little stir in the passersby. From her place in the shadows she hears them saying "He *is* coming! He *is* coming!"

The street becomes so crowded that no one even notices her. She drops to her knees and crawls toward the center of the mob. Slowly she edges closer. Never has she been so determined. Everything is on the line today.

The people bump her and step on her fingers and toes, but she is silent. If they notice who is creeping in they would immediately take her to the priest. She, is after all, unclean, but she doesn't dare announce it. No one would understand why she needed to touch the Rabbi. No one would even give her a chance to explain. She would be stoned to death.

Slowly she edges toward Him. She is risking every-thing on one touch. No matter what, live or die, she refuses to remain the same.

The laughter and chatter of the crowd seem to mock her. It is as though the world goes on without her. All seem impervious to her desperation. Even when they step on her or trip over her, they ignore her.

Folks, we live in an hour of desperation. People are coming to church, playing the game and leaving as empty or even emptier. We are not touching them at the point of their pain. We offer substitutes of good music, positive, encouraging preaching and successful administration. We tell them to study more, as if more knowledge will add to their faith and they can be like us. We pretend to have answers when the truth is much of the ministry is strongly considering suicide or at least immediate resignation. Even they don't seem to be able to find peace.

The hour has come for honesty. Let's ask the hard

questions. Let's drink from the cup we offer to others. Either the claims of the gospel are true or they are not. If the gospel is nothing more than a pack of clever lies weaved into a convincing story, I would rather know now. Will anything happen if we connect with Jesus?

Finally the woman spies the colorful hem and tassels of Jesus' tallith, the prayer shawl that symbolizes relationship, truth, unity and presence. She touches it and suddenly Jesus stops in His tracks. "Who touched Me?" He asks.

Her hopes of quickly withdrawing are gone. No one moves. He spoke with such authority the crowd is stunned. No one answers.

Slowly everyone backs away as one of the disciples says, "Lord, there are so many. Anyone could have bumped into You."

"No!" Jesus says. "Someone who was hungry got hold of My promises. Who is it?"

A gasp comes from the crowd. As they inch back they left the woman exposed to everyone's gaze. This is the woman that they have used as an example of the futility of secret sin. This is the woman whose only purpose in life lately has been to be used as an example, a bad example, to the children. And now she has done the unthinkable.

Before anyone can say anything else, she admits her crime. She is simply honest. Oh how refreshing it would be for the church to simply admit that something has gone wrong. We cannot possibly expect people to believe that we are the same church as the one in the book of Acts. Something is missing.

Jesus says, "Yes, sister, I knew it was you all along. I don't refuse the hungry. Your belief that I would respond to your heart's agony is rewarded. You are whole."

I cannot believe that Jesus would do less for us if we reach out to touch Him. The hour is upon us for honest examination. Get hungry, saints. There is more on the table than what we have tasted. True spiritual hunger is a willingness to lay everything on the line for just one touch. But it is the touch of God. It's how we got into the church to begin with. We came to an altar and laid it all on the line. This will never be replaced by great large edifices and fine choirs. Education will never be an adequate substitute.

"Is it enough?" you ask. It is the touch that satisfies. If you read Matthew 14:35–36, you will see what I mean.

> And when the men of that place had knowledge of him, they sent out into all that country round about, and brought unto him all that were diseased; And besought him that they might only touch the hem of his garment: and as many as touched were made perfectly whole (KJV).

This is how Jesus was received about a mile down the road from where the woman was healed. Everyone had heard of the woman's testimony, and they all wanted to touch Him just as she did. He is not a God who rejects the hungry.

> "Blessed are they which do hunger and thirst after righteousness: for they shall be filled."
> —Matthew 5:6, KJV

I'm still hungry, church. Are you?

Chapter 5

The Hireling Mentality

THERE WAS A MAN who lived in a graveyard. The city had once been his home. But now the demoniac of Gadara claimed the surrounding cliffs and their tombs as his place. He was so tormented that he was self-destructive, cutting his body with the sharp stones that littered the stark landscape. He was empowered by rage and hysteria to such a degree that chains wouldn't hold him. (See Mark 5.)

The storm of one night in particular rivaled the storm in this man's heart. I can see him on top of a rock naked and howling, screams piercing the rain-soaked night and drifting down to the little village below. Children hide under their beds, and fathers rise to check the bolts and latches at doors and windows.

Suddenly in the middle of this commotion there falls a thundering silence. The wind stops. The rain ceases. I can picture the demoniac atop his rock,

40

silent, startled into peace. Dumbfounded and shocked he surveys the landscape. The sun is just creeping over the horizon.

He spots a fisherman's boat landing on shore with several men on board, but one is different. There is something about Him. His demon-crazed mind doesn't know what to think or how to sort it out, but something in him connects with the supernatural peace that surrounds him with this Man.

He leaps from his perch and begins to run stumbling and sliding down the hill. When the disciples spot him, fear fills their hearts. The reputation of this man is no small thing. The disciples had tried to talk Jesus out of even landing here.

As the demoniac approaches within a few yards of Jesus, he falls to his knees and slides in at Jesus' feet to worship Him. Here is a man with between two and six thousand demons, and yet they cannot stop him from worshipping. It makes one wonder what it is that stops us.

You probably know the rest of the story. Jesus confronted the demons, who begged to go into the herd of swine. Jesus consented. The pigs preferred death to demonic possession. They commit "sooie-cide" by leaping into the sea. (This is the first historical reference to deviled ham, by the way.)

The townspeople find out their pigs are dead, and they are incensed. It is of little importance to them that a life has been changed. There seems to be no thought for the man who has been delivered. They are upset about the money they have lost.

Many churches would respond the same way. Keeping their tithing pigs is far more important than a homeless, jobless, demon-possessed person receiving deliverance. Most of our churches would much rather offend the newborn baby convert than that mean, old tither. It's all a matter of economics, you know. We all know that God expects us to keep those tithers. How else will His church survive financially? We certainly don't want to have to depend on our faith.

Then the man who is delivered wants to go with Jesus. He loves the thrill of being in church. He enjoys the security he has found in God's presence.

But Jesus quickly lets him know that his personal comfort isn't the priority. He sends him back home as a witness. Others are the mission. It isn't our comfort, convenience and entertainment that Jesus died to provide. It is to make us part of His army for taking back souls from Satan. Depopulating hell is our crusade. The church must be stirred. It must wake up. America is depending on us.

BIBLICAL ORDER

Why doesn't today's church follow Jesus' orders to go forth and tell of God's compassion to those who haven't heard? The problems of churches in the United States are many and varied, but I believe they all fit under one category; that is, a lack of true biblical order.

Because most Christians have no idea what biblical order is. I'm going to start by explaining how we can identify it in Scripture. Then we will look at the first precepts of order God establishes in Genesis 1:1, which are unity and relationship. Finally we'll see what Jesus said about levels of relationship.

UNDERSTANDING BIBLICAL ORDER

If any order is to be called biblical, it must have certain characteristics:

1. Simplicity
2. Verification in Scripture as a whole

Many have attempted to discover biblical order by taking one incident in the Word or one occasion and then practicing that small portion and expecting the same miraculous results. This has often brought about a small successful result but not anything like what was expected.

Paul wrote to both Corinth and Rome about simplicity.

> . . . he that giveth, let him do it with simplicity . . .
>
> —ROMANS 12:8, KJV

> For our rejoicing is this, the testimony of our conscience, that in simplicity and godly sincerity, not with fleshly wisdom, but by the grace of God, we have had our conversation in the world, and more abundantly to youward.
>
> —2 CORINTHIANS 1:12, KJV

> But I fear, lest by any means, as the serpent beguiled Eve through his subtilty, so your minds should be corrupted from the simplicity that is in Christ.
>
> —2 CORINTHIANS 11:3, KJV

Science, as we know it, originally was established as a study to prove the existence of God. This ended when it was still in its infancy. Although the elements of the natural world are complex with layer upon layer, they are very simple at their most basic level. God is divine in His simplicity. He never tries to prove to His creation how complex He is.

The gospel is simply amazing in its simplicity. Jesus even said that faith must resemble that of a child for a person to enter into heaven.

With all this in mind, the order of God can be recognized by its simplicity. It must also be a thread you can trace from Genesis to Revelation. If you were to see a miraculous result in Scripture and wish to achieve that same result, then you must understand that there are deeper principals then the circumstances of that one incident.

Don't ever forget that every story you read in Scripture was set in the context of a whole culture. Jesus gave a key to understanding the miracles of His ministry when He said, "Think not that I am come to destroy the law, or the prophets: I am not come to destroy, but to fulfill. For verily I say unto you, Till heaven and earth pass, one jot or one tittle shall in no wise pass from the law, till all be fulfilled" (Matt. 5:17–18, KJV).

Jesus' comment was pointed at the way Pharisees and/or Sadducees argued about the Torah (the first five books of the Old Testament). If one were considered guilty of misquoting—or more often misappropriating and misinterpreting—the Word he would be accused of "destroying Torah."

Jesus said, "I haven't come to destroy the law or even quote and apply it properly. I have come to fulfill." That is, He came to be the fulfillment of what had been taught. Jesus built every statement and act upon what the Jews had been taught since they were children. He operated in His own culture. The reason we see Pharisees warning Him about Herod's threats (Luke 13:31) and someone like Nicodemus coming to Jesus and saying, "We know you're the one sent from God" (John 3:2) is that Jesus operated within the culture of the Pharisees and the law, but in a radical way.

Many nations of the world change Jesus to suit them and their respective culture. Never forget Christianity is a mid-Eastern mystic religion at its roots. Otherwise there would be no understanding of terms like the *Holy Spirit*.

Keeping all of this in mind, look at the Hebrew word for truth. It is pronounced eh'-meth but it has only three Hebrew letters. The first is a*lpha*, which is also the first letter of the Hebrew alphabet. Alpha is the first letter of the word *truth* because if it's not true in the beginning, it never is true, no matter how it appears.

The second letter is *mem*, which is the middle letter of the Hebrew alphabet. This symbolizes if it's not true now, it wasn't true in the beginning and it won't be true in the end.

The third letter is *tav*, the last letter in the Hebrew alphabet. If it isn't true in the end, it wasn't true in the beginning or the middle.

Order doesn't just appear in one context. It is seen from Genesis to Revelation or it isn't God's set and ordained order.

All this working together then we know that God's order will be simple and will be found throughout the Word.

Let's go to Genesis 1:1. We can see two precepts of

God's order exhibited in this very first scripture, and these elements can be seen all the way through to Revelation.

RELATIONSHIP AND UNITY

The first precept is *relationship*. "In the beginning God." In this verse, the Hebrew word for God is *Elohym*, which is the plural of *Elowehh*. In the very first phrase of the very first verse of Scripture we find relationship—Father, Son and Holy Ghost working together.

It is easy then to understand that God working in us begins with relationship—our relationship with Him and our relationship with others.

The second element of order I bring to your attention is in fact considered by many scholars to be the most basic and most profound of all principles. It is *unity*.

The Jews have what they call the *Shema*. It is a quote from Deuteronomy 6:4.

> Hear, O Israel: The Lord our God is one Lord.

If you take the time to search the Word you will find relationship and unity everywhere. They are truly basic. In fact, without them you will find chaos and death, whether it be a church, a relationship with God or the functioning of God Himself. It is capsulized by God in Hebrews 13:8, "Jesus Christ the same yesterday, and today and for ever."

Someone once said that what this literally means is Jesus has one foot in yesterday, because He is in yesterday now. His other foot is in tomorrow, because He is in tomorrow now. And He is straddling today. There is no shadow of turning. He is one with all things. He is in full relationship with all things, even time itself. These principles are immutable and unchanging. We must walk in them to have the blessing of God on our lives.

When you look at the patriarchs, relationship and unity are evidenced. Abraham, Isaac and Jacob actively sought a relationship with an unknown God. They didn't have a Bible to tell them about God, and they came after God when no one else on the planet was doing so.

But when we get to the New Testament instead of man seeking God we find a God who is so hungry for relationship, He is coming after us. I'm so glad He did. But the truth is that even in the Old Testament God was hungry for relationship with His creation. He was so hungry that He brought the flood on people who totally rejected Him so that the earth could be repopulated with people who would seek Him.

Looking at the teachings of Jesus, I should also see God's desire for relationship. Now we'll look specifically at Jesus' clearest teachings on levels of relationship with God.

THE HIRELING

The best example of Jesus' teaching on the first level of relationship with God is derived from John 10, "I am the good shepherd. The good shepherd gives His life for the sheep. But a hireling, he who is not the shepherd, one who does not own the sheep, sees the wolf coming and leaves the sheep and flees; and the wolf catches the sheep and scatters them" (John 10:11–12, NKJV). We know that Jesus is the Good Shepherd. We also know Satan is the wolf. But who is the hireling? It has to be you and I.

Let me explain. A hireling is very simply someone without commitment to relationship or ownership in the company. He is not a bad person. Quite the contrary. He may be a good person as a whole and a good worker. He may have integrity and a fair sense of responsibility. In fact, he is probably the kind of person every employer is looking to hire.

But there is one problem, just one chink in the spiritual armor, one fatal flaw for the overseer. A hireling works with an expectation of a payday. It is his focus.

You might think that this isn't really a problem. But if you were his employer and he were offered a better payday someplace else, you would certainly think differently. Hirelings have wallet loyalty. Their loyalty and effort are directly connected to their employer's ability to supply remuneration.

There isn't anything evil about this. After all, this is how God got each one of us into the kingdom. We each came to a point in life where we offered ourselves to Jesus, and in return we expected total forgiveness and sonship. As a bonus we found out that there was an incredible retirement program for those who stayed with the company. The problem with this is that you cannot build a real relationship on this criteria.

The end result is a person who does everything they do with a payday in mind. They will fast so long as it gets them something they couldn't achieve by eating. They pray in response to their own needs. They will go to church so long as the sermons or choir are entertaining enough. Everything they do for Jesus is based on the expectations of return. Nothing is done with consistency or passion unless it gives an immediate personal return.

This hireling syndrome is the prevalent attitude in the American church. I believe it is the major reason that we have hundreds of thousands of churches in America that have less than one hundred in attendance on the average Sunday morning. I know this statement calls for further explanation.

A congregation with a prevalent hireling mindset expects payday from God. They believe the total purpose of the church and its ministry is to meet their personal needs whether supposed or real. This belief is the exact diametric opposite of the gospel. Jesus said after we receive we must give it away (Matt. 10:8).

The scriptural purpose of the church is very simply to reach the lost and then disciple and mature them to reach the lost. It is a "go ye" relationship with Jesus. The hireling church is a terrible perversion of everything we were designed to become.

It is unscriptural for a church to be totally designed for the comfort, pleasure and ease of those already attending. In these churches a visitor cannot easily become an integral part. They must elbow their way into a closed society. The very people the church is to reach cannot get in without a struggle. It is the travesty of the ages. In fact, if a new Christian is radically fresh and on fire, attempting to operate as scripturally as possible, then in most cases he or she must backslide to get along with those already in church. Many long-time Christians develop a condescending attitude to new believers, calling it patience. "Mature" Christians know if they wait and don't mentor or stoke the fire, a new convert will become just like them. That is, of course, unless the new convert becomes so disillusioned he just quits.

If the new convert quits, the church people just nod their heads knowingly, without accepting their responsibility for their lack of action. Many even blame God! No wonder the Holy Spirit is so careful about where He draws the unsaved, lest they become "twice more the sons of hell" (Matt. 23:15).

As a pastor, I hate to admit that this focus on pleasing those already in the church is consistently contributed to by those in ministry. Many of those entering ministry soon conclude that if you aren't finding emotional gratification from those in your church then you are obviously failing God. Since God is invisible, the proof of your being a good minister of the gospel is in how highly the people already in the church think of you. Even if the church is dead, twice dead, three times dead and no one has been saved or changed in years, the minister feels that he has to get along with them to please God. If a pastor decides to do something to displease a church with this mentality, he'll pay for it. I learned that lesson the hard way.

LEARNING THE HARD WAY

I was in one of my early pastorates in a small town. The church offered me thirty-five dollars a week pay. There was no parsonage, so I had to rent a place for my family and me. I had three children ranging in ages between seven and eleven years. I, of course, had to take a job locally at minimum wage just to pay the rent and eat.

The church was housed in a small building with gas

heaters and lots of mildew. It was just a block building, so the temperature outside was sorely felt inside.

When I arrived, the congregation had been without a pastor for seventeen months. Only nine adults attended, and not all of those were attending regularly. One family did have three children, so that meant if all came we had twelve in attendance, not counting the five from my own house. At least I got a unanimous vote to take the pastorate.

I had been there two weeks preaching my heart out and working twelve hours a day on a job to survive. Not a single comment had been made about my preaching. Finally, being young and foolish, I said something to them as they were crowding around for fellowship following a Sunday night service. Boy, was that a mistake.

One of the board members put his arm around my shoulders and said, "Pastor, we didn't call you here because we like your preaching. We don't like your preaching, but you were the only one who would take this church."

To say the least, I was devastated. What in the world was going on? Was this the way the church was to be?

Near the end of the summer the air conditioner broke down. It was going to cost over five hundred dollars to fix, so I called an emergency board meeting.

Everyone on the board came from two-income families, and some were executives in local companies. I naturally figured it wouldn't be a problem to get the money together. I told them that I had arranged to borrow fifty dollars from a relative out of state. I thought if each of them could give fifty dollars or so we could get the rest out of what little treasury we had.

One of the board members stood, cleared his throat and began to speak. He said in essence that he was sure that everyone, including the pastor, understood that the air conditioning was part of the church, just like the pastor was part of the church. This being so, he explained, it was obvious that the repair of the air conditioners would have to come out of my salary.

I was stunned. I just sat there for a minute. Then pulling together what little wits I had, I responded. I told them basically that at my current rate of pay I would have to pastor them almost four months just to pay for the air, and I didn't know if I could let my family suffer that long, so I guess they would just have to sit and sweat at church. And we all did.

Every year in the fall the congregation would take a vacation for three weeks. The whole church. They went camping. The former pastor had gone with them and held church where they camped. They just closed the church for those three weekends. I was dumbfounded.

I told them I couldn't and wouldn't do that. I couldn't take three weeks off because I needed to work my secular job so that my family could eat. I also told them *I didn't work for them*. I worked for Jesus. My responsibility wasn't just to them, but to the lost all around us. I had to stay and have church if I only preached to my family.

They all left and went camping. In the meantime the Holy Spirit spoke to me in prayer. He told me to go door-to-door in an apartment complex. I had done that before and I have done it since, but never have I gotten the response I got in this instance.

The first Sunday the congregation was gone we had twenty visitors. Seven adults got saved. This church hadn't seen anyone saved since one of the board members was saved four years previously. It was a miracle.

The Sunday morning before the congregation went on vacation there had been sixteen in Sunday school, counting my family. The first Sunday they came back we had fifty-four. I was on cloud nine, but they were very upset. They did *not* like the change.

During this time a furniture store next door to the church made some inquiries about buying our building. We even went to meet with them—"we" meaning the board and I. But they weren't offering us near the money we would need to relocate so I just let it go.

Soon the church was doing well. It was growing. We had new converts, and I had dreams of a church of sixty continuing to grow until it took the city. I know I was naive, but when people are being saved and changed it is easy for me to dream and believe.

The first Wednesday night in December after church, one of the board members approached me. I should have known something was up. He had begun his conversation by complimenting my sermon. This hadn't happened to this point previously.

He told me that we needed to have a church business meeting. I felt like they wanted to get rid of me. They were not pleased with all the changes brought by growth. I was going to take in members in another week, so I knew if we operated by the bylaws everything would be all right. According to the church bylaws you couldn't have an official church business meeting without announcing it on two Sundays previous to the meeting, so I responded with that information.

The board members told me to shut up and sit down because I was now, presently, at that very moment, in the meeting. I slowly sank down on the altar next to me as one gentleman proceeded to inform me that they, the board, had sold the building. In fact they had already closed the deal and split the money up between the five families. They were just letting me know that December 23 was our last Sunday in that building.

Now I don't want you to get the wrong impression about my ministry. This is the only congregation that ever resigned on me. It's very hard to describe the emotions that ran through me. I felt hollow and empty. I wondered what had gone wrong—how I had failed the church. I spent the next couple of weeks getting my new converts into other churches. Our last Sunday was Christmas Sunday, and no one attended except my own family.

I went home upset and defeated. But I told my wife that I didn't work for the church. They had no control of me. I belonged to Jesus Christ. He had called me to Himself and assigned me duties, and my work was the fulfilling of relationship responsibilities. If the whole world and every deacon rejected me it had no bearing on my life in Jesus. I must keep my attitude right and my life clean. That was it. I must add, though, that most of my bravado was for her because inside I felt empty, rejected and like a total failure. She did well in bolstering my bruised spirit and ego.

We were broke. It was Christmas, and I didn't get paid by the church. But two things happened. They both came by telephone. The first was a call from another church. They wanted me to try out the next Sunday. I did and was voted in. I never missed a Sunday. God is good!

The second was from a family we had pastored previously. They told us they were driving over the next morning with a financial love offering and a set of tires for my car, which I needed desperately. Only God can provide in such a manner.

HIRELING CHURCHES

Hireling churches such as the one I have just described are that way because they have been discipled by hireling ministry. These are leaders of insecurity, trying to create a secure environment in an insecure world. The result is a ministry that shows the greatest honor to those with the best education, largest crowds and most ornate facilities. There is no honor for simple obedience to the gospel, self-sacrifice or relationship with God. I should say there is no honor unless they leave the country and do it overseas. I wonder how much of this has to do with those ministers no longer being a threat to those who remain in America.

Visible, tangible success becomes the criterion for honor. Their greatness is measured by their physical accomplishments. Oratorical skills are far more important than anointing or passion. In fact oratorical skills, pulpit mannerisms and the ability to entertain are soon mistaken for the anointing by a people with no real prayer lives of their own.

Another factor in the creation of hireling ministry is that many of those who are entering ministry are very emotionally immature. They need to be needed. They can't mature and nurture a congregation. They mother it instead. In doing so, they become controlling and manipulative.

In order to nurture you must be willing to give people whatever is necessary for their personal growth and maturity. This means that there are times for encouragement and accolades, but there are also times for correction and discipline. Ice cream is good, but Brussels sprouts are better for you. I'm not talking about abuse, but I am referring to balance.

It can be personally gratifying when people need and depend upon you and your personal involvement during crisis. But if you are not careful, they stop differentiating between minor problems and major crises. Soon the pastor is doing their praying, Bible study and witnessing. He's even running around solving their minor personality conflicts. After all, isn't that what they pay the pastor to do? Isn't that why they *hired* him?

Today the pastor often works *for the church* not *with Jesus*. The church board controls his salary, job description and his eternal destiny. If the minister doesn't please and obey them they will just hire another. A church without a biblical foundation operates from the congregation up. It doesn't matter what God wants or decrees in His eternal word. The will of the congregation must be obeyed. God's way is tolerated at best and in many cases perverted. In fact, in most churches God isn't even given a vote. Nothing operates on "it seemed good to the Holy Ghost, and to us" (Acts 15:28, KJV). Everything operates on what seems good to us. The whole of church government and activities operates around how well the core of the church is pleased and how well the people in the pew are taken care of. This kind of church doesn't even remotely resemble the intentions of its Creator.

All this is due to a hireling mentality. The average church can best be described as hireling pastors hired by hireling churches. It amounts to a church that blesses itself, serves the saved and thus keeps the saved saved while the world goes to hell. It's a church operated by petty temper tantrums rather than divine biblical order and authority.

The Lord must weep. He birthed an entity through His own sacrifice, suffering, death and resurrection only to see it evolve into a deformed child. The church is designed and equipped for power, yet impotent. Compared to its first one hundred years, it's a mere shadow. A church that once witnessed the miraculous on a daily basis now sees so few healings that even one that is medically verified becomes a television sensation.

The church staggers about in a daze. She looks for shortcuts and formulas, ready to grasp any new idea that will return her to her former glory and power. She prefers one new method that will miraculously cure all her troubles. Meanwhile most mainline denominations are shrinking at an ever-increasing and alarming rate.

I personally know of at least one denomination that has put a freeze on the removal of members' names who have left the church—even if they have left by death. All this is so that statistically they won't lose ground.

This is totally unnecessary. We have been given a power beyond anything we have imagined. Excuses and slight of hand with statistics only encourage the move away from the supernatural. Jesus is everything the Bible says He is. If we will turn our hearts toward truth and exercise the gifts within us, the church can be restored to first-century power.

Chapter 6

The Church's Opportunity to Repent

HOW CAN A HIRELING be changed? We can see the answer in the writings of the sons of Korah. To really understand what they wrote, we need to know about their infamous father, Korah.

Korah was one of the Levites who left Egypt with the rest of the children of Israel. He probably wasn't such a bad guy, but he wasn't good at picking friends. His were two guys who had been Moses' thorns from the beginning. It was Dathan and Abiram, two men of the tribe of Reuben. You can find the story in Numbers 16.

Now this tribe always had problems. Remember the mixed blessing of their father, Jacob, before he died.

> Reuben, you are my firstborn, my might, the beginning (the firstfruits) of my manly strength and vigor; [your birthright gave

you] the preeminence in dignity and the preeminence in power. But unstable and boiling
over like water, you shall not excel and have
the preeminence [of the firstborn], because
you went to your father's bed; you defiled
it—he went to my couch!

—GENESIS 49:3–4, AMP.

Dathan and Abiram fit right in with the dubious
heritage of their tribe. Though they had no authority
outside of their tribe, they knew how to flatter, manip-
ulate and control. They worked on the two hundred
and fifty princes of the tribe of Israel. They also
needed someone who had some right to confront
Moses and Aaron. That's why they got Korah.

Korah was a Levite. They began to plant ideas in
his mind about Moses' nepotism. After all who was
Moses to say that only his brother and nephews could
offer incense?

When Korah and the two hundred and fifty princes
offered incense, fire fell from heaven and devoured
them (Num. 16:35; 26:10). Where were the instiga-
tors—Dathan and Abiram? They stayed at their tents
and let others do their dirty work. But God knew. The
ground under their tents opened up and swallowed
them and their children as they stood to watch the
show (Num. 16:23–33).

But a strange thing took place. Although Numbers
16 says that the families of Dathan and Abiram per-
ished with them, Numbers 26:11 states that Korah's
children did not perish with them. In fact, oral tradition states that as their father is confronting Moses
they were in intercession asking Jehovah for mercy.
And, of course, it was given.

THE REDEEMED SONS

Now these sons of Korah wanted everyone to know that mercy was possible and that God could redeem any name. So they weren't known by their own names but as the redeemed sons of a malefactor.

And the sons of Korah knew what it was to be outsiders, so they could empathize with David as they wrote Psalm 84 about his exile. But this psalm speaks to the heart of anyone in exile, from Israelite refugees to the New Testament church.

The whole sense of the psalm is spiritual relationship and hunger. (This is a familiar theme in the Psalms, particularly Psalms 42, 63, portions of 73, 119 and 143.)

Using a metaphor with birds, this psalm shows us how God will respond when a hireling seeks a deeper relationship with Him. When Israel was being taunted by her enemies, they would refer to her as a wild bird. When wild birds have their nests raided by a predator they would find a new nest. Israel was being chided for the fact that when anything went wrong they would find another God. They would leave the nest of Zion.

But the sons of Korah turned that insult around. They wrote:

> Even the sparrow has found a home,
> And the swallow a nest for herself,
> Where she may lay her young—
> Even Your altars, O Lord of hosts,
> My King and my God.
>
> —PSALM 84:3, NKJV

Though Israel appeared to be like a sparrow or

swallow—wild birds—she had done something the dove would do. After the nest is raided the dove returns to start over. After her time in exile, Israel returned to the altar of the Lord to start over.

The sons of Korah are saying we are nesting near the altar of sacrifice. In fact, verse 5, speaks of the highways of Zion, and the devout Jews believe that every highway of Zion leads to God's altar. In this present hour God is speaking to His church to return to the altar. Sometimes it wouldn't hurt to get saved and baptized in the Holy Spirit all over again. Ezekiel captures this thought. He says two times under the unction of the Holy Spirit: "turn ye, turn ye from your evil ways" (Ezek. 33:11, KJV). We must turn!

Many who are seeking revival quote 2 Chronicles 7:14. But it is as though they think it is a magic formula rather than a commandment with a promise.

> If My people, who are called by My name, shall humble themselves, pray, seek, crave, and require of necessity My face and turn from their wicked ways, then will I hear from heaven, forgive their sin, and heal their land (Amp.).

We must humble ourselves, not wait to be humbled. We must seek and require His face not His hand, and we must turn! Turn from the comfort of church as usual! Turn from man pleasing to Holy Ghost hunger! Turn from cultivated gifts and talents to the precious anointing. Turn, turn for this is the season for the Holy Ghost and love on fire.

THE SEASON OF LOVE ON FIRE

Jeremiah said he didn't really want to do it. It would be much easier to be quiet and not utter a word against the secularized church. But Jeremiah wrote:

> His word was in mine heart as a burning fire shut up in my bones, and I was weary with forbearing, and I could not stay.
> —JEREMIAH 20:9, KJV

The Amplified Bible says the fire was shut up in his mind and heart. Either way it is a fire that burns in the innermost part of a man. I am on fire with hunger to the bone. And I never want to go out. Search me, O Lord. The only good thing about me is You. I know where I have come from. None of us are really any good without You. We need Your fiery love.

Though Jeremiah had fire in his bones, he was distraught over the words of judgment he had to speak against the religious. This is what it means to have "love on fire."

> Concerning the prophets: My heart [says Jeremiah] is broken within me, all my bones shake: I am like a drunken man, a man whom wine has overcome, because of the Lord and because of His holy words [which He has pronounced against unfaithful leaders].
> —JEREMIAH. 23:9, AMP.

Love on fire burns to call the church back to purpose. God has a purpose and mission for every people of every time.

> For a long time now—to this very day—you
> have not deserted your brothers but have
> carried out the mission the Lord your God
> gave you.
> —JOSHUA 22:3, NIV

God declares the end or destiny of a thing before its beginning.

> Declaring the end *and* the result from the
> beginning, and from ancient times the
> things that are not yet done, saying, My
> counsel shall stand, and I will do all My plea-
> sure *and* purpose.
> —ISAIAH 46:10, AMP.

In other words, before you were created God looked into the future and saw what He desired you to become. At your creation He put in you everything you needed to get you there. Then at salvation those seeds of destiny burst into life.

He did the same for the church. He planted seeds of destiny and watered the seeds with His own blood. In every local assembly that marches toward its destiny God brings to life the very gifts that will get it there. They will be added to us as we journey and grow. God will see that we are joined by every person and gifting that will be required by our destiny.

Most churches don't have because they honestly don't need. They can adequately supply what men require of them, so they do not pursue what God intends for them. They are going nowhere and don't need anything additional from God to get them there.

Leaving the church in the hands of man may appear

to be a fatal flaw in God's plan. But the truth is that He left it in the hands of man that they should in humility surrender it to the design and will of God.

Read the book. God will have a last-day church of relationship and revival. I know it will be. I know as Daniel did that the time is upon us. And like Daniel my cry is simply, "Please, Lord, don't do it without me."

THE GOOD EYE AND THE EVIL EYE

For today's church to break the hireling mentality that now possesses it, we must get our eyes off ourselves and circumstances. We must turn back to what we are really all about—others. The question is, will we be givers or takers? The Bible speaks to this issue using the Hebrew idiom of good eyes and evil eyes.

We still use this idiom today in common speech when it comes to choosing someone with expertise to do some work or to look at a project. We will say, "Let so-and-so look at it. He has a good eye for that kind of thing."

The Book of Proverbs speaks of eyes in both the positive and negative sense. In the negative sense it is translated as having an "evil eye." An evil eye isn't what our modern speech allows it to be. It isn't an ability to cast some kind of necromantic or witchcraft spell, nor the ability to hypnotize. Even though the modern meaning is caught up in psychics and tarot cards, an evil eye has absolutely nothing to do with these things.

This evil eye is spoken of in Proverbs 23:6:

Eat thou not the bread of him that hath an

> evil eye, neither desire thou his dainty meats
> (KJV).

> Eat not the bread of him who has a hard,
> grudging, and envious eye, neither desire his
> dainty foods (Amp).

The Amplified is clearest in its translation. The evil eye is a hard, grudging, envious eye.

Literally if the man with an evil eye does anything for you it's with real motive of what he can get from you. But the end result is that you would gladly give up what you have received in order to be free of him. Again we read in Proverbs 28:22:

> He that hasteth to be rich hath an evil eye,
> and considereth not that poverty shall come
> upon him (KJV).

The Amplified Bible calls it an evil and covetous eye. The evil eye is the eye that sees everything through the attitude of covetousness. What can I get from this person or situation?

It is the eye of the hireling. It finds itself organizing its thinking into what will be advantageous for me or mine. It never does anything without motive. It only gives to receive, does to receive, works to receive and so forth. Whether it be tithe or church work, if they aren't going to receive they will not give. There is no thought of doing for others unless we are at least going to get our rightful recognition. Sometimes accolades and titles in these cases can be as valuable as dollars and sense.

In America we think that an evil eye is related to the

casting of spells in witchcraft. Our thinking on this may arise from the traditional belief that the attitude of an evil eye always attracts demon activity.

On the other hand, Proverbs also speaks of the good or bountiful or whole eye.

> He that hath a bountiful eye shall be blessed;
> for he giveth of his bread to the poor.
> —Proverbs. 22:9

Other scriptures that relate are Proverbs 11:25, 19:17 and 21:3, and Psalm 41:1–3. They speak of God's provision for those who give generously to others.

It seems that scripturally if a church has a bountiful eye it doesn't have to worry. God will see it through any trouble.

We find this in the New Testament also. Jesus uses the "good eye" phrase in Matthew 6:22. The King James translates it as "single" eye, but the NIV more accurately translates the Greek word *haplous* as "whole." But it is the Jewish bountiful eye. This whole portion of Scripture from verse 14 to verse 23 and even beyond speaks of giving and doing for the Master, in such varied ways as forgiving others, fasting and storing up treasure in heaven.

Many have interpreted this verse to mean focus and single-mindednes, but that isn't it at all. It would be better to go to James 1:6–8 for that. Single-minded focus is very, very important, but it isn't what Matthew 6:22 is speaking of. In this passage Jesus is speaking of our attitude when we see others. The "good eye" is an attitude that says, "What can I add to this person or project?" rather than, "What will I get?"

Jesus refers to the negative side in Matthew 5:29, regarding an eye that offends or brings us into reproach. Jesus says it is better to pluck it out.

Again we see it in Matthew 20:15 when Jesus says;

> Is it not lawful for me to do what I will with my own? Is thine eye evil, because I am good? (KJV).

The Amplified adds, "Or do you begrudge my being generous?"

Jesus was teaching a parable about a man who sent laborers into the field. The man was questioned by those who went in early about how he rewarded those He sent in late.

The evil eye is jealous and always looking out for itself. It is in competition with every other worker in the field.

Matthew 6:23 says our light becomes darkness if we have an evil eye. Truly today's church has become a place of darkness and poverty when it comes to the manifest power and glory of God. But then it's only fair because we are hirelings, and, as Romans 6:23 states, we are simply collecting our wages.

> For from within, out of the heart of men, proceed evil thoughts, adulteries, fornications, murders, thefts, covetousness, wickedness, deceit, lasciviousness, an *evil eye*, blasphemy, pride, foolishness: all these evil things come from within, and defile the man.
> —MARK 7:21–23, KJV, EMPHASIS ADDED

These are what defile the man and—may I add

without changing its intent—the church also since it is made up of basically human beings.

The Bible states that good eye or evil eye, we are going to be confronted.

> Behold, He is coming with the clouds, and every eye will see Him, even those who pierced Him; and all the tribes of the earth shall gaze upon Him and beat their breasts and mourn and lament over Him. Even so [must it be]. Amen (so be it).
> —Revelation 1:7, Amp.

The truth to us should be that the value of people isn't in what they can do for us but in what Jesus has already done for them. Jesus went to the cross for them. It is referred to in Scripture as "the joy that was set before him" (Heb. 12:2, KJV).

The purpose of Jesus was to reach the lost. It is now the purpose of the church. It is the reward Jesus receives for what He did. And He is worthy of the reward of His suffering.

The matter doesn't rest on whether or not a person deserves Jesus. No one does, and, for that matter, neither do we. But the fact remains that He is worthy of His reward.

I must spend my life reaching the lost because He is worthy!—not to mention the fact He was sent to purchase me.

So long as He is worthy I must be about the business of salvation. He . . . is . . . worthy!

GOD'S INTENTION FOR THE CHURCH

So you can see that God's intention is very different from the self-centered hireling church. He has laid careful plans and a priceless foundation. He looked to and longed for this hour.

> For I know the thoughts *and* plans that I have for you, says the Lord, thoughts *and* plans for welfare *and* peace and not for evil, to give you hope in your final outcome.
> —JEREMIAH 29:11, AMP., ITALICS ADDED

Every design of God is good and perfect. The welfare of all is always His intent. He told us specifically that because of the provision of intercession by the Holy Ghost that all things work together for good, no matter what Satan throws at me or you (Rom. 8:26–28).

There is a scripture in Deuteronomy I love. It is a plain and powerful promise.

> The eternal God is your refuge *and* dwelling place, and underneath are the everlasting arms; He drove the enemy before you *and* thrust them out, saying, Destroy!
> —DEUTERONOMY 33:27, AMP.

I am told that the Hebrew word used for "underneath" is the same as the word for "the floor of a wine press." It most literally means that no matter what Satan sends to hold me down it only presses me into Jesus. I cannot lose. Throw your best shot, Satan. All you accomplish is for me to be deeper in Him. Hallelujah!

Because of the Holy Spirit groaning in my behalf I am blessed, no matter what. Everything has been designed for my welfare. Even the structure we know as the local church has a purpose. We are a "one-another" fellowship. We fit the first principle of biblical order—relationship.

The phrase "one another" appears forty-one times in the New Testament (King James Version). We are to:

Love one another: John 13:34, 15:12, 17; Romans 13:8; 1 Thessalonians 4:9; 1 Peter 1:22; 1 John 3:11, 23, 4:11–12; and 2 John 1:5

Excuse one another: Romans 2:15

Prefer one another: Romans 12:10

Receive one another: Romans 15:7

Admonish one another: Romans 15:14

Salute one another with a holy kiss: Romans 16:16, 2 Corinthians 13:12 and 1 Peter 5:14

Serve one another: Galatians 5:13

Bear one another's burdens: Galatians 6:2

Forebear one another: Ephesians 4:2, Colossians 3:13

Forgive one another: Ephesians 4:32, Colossians 3:13

Admonish one another: Colossians 3:16

Comfort one another: 1 Thessalonians 4:18

Edify one another: 1 Thessalonians 5:11

Exhort one another: Hebrews 3:13, 10:25

Consider one another to provoke unto love and to good works: Hebrews 10:24

The church was designed for the benefit of all. That is why Paul basically writes in Hebrews 10:25—Don't you dare get in the habit of missing church.

SUMMARY

In this chapter we have seen the following ways a local church or an individual believer can repent for staying in the hireling relationship so long.

1. Return to the altar of sacrifice.
2. Humble themselves.
3. Seek God's face.
4. Pursue God's purpose—reaching the lost.
5. Focus their eyes on others—not themselves.

God doesn't leave us to take these steps on our own. He confronts us in ways I will describe in the next chapter.

Chapter 7

How God Confronts Us

EVERYTHING GOD HAS done is to benefit others. Now He is waiting for us to remove the mind of a hireling and put on the mind of Christ (1 Cor. 2:16). Jesus warns the church at Thyatira to never forget that He is the one who "searches minds (the thoughts, feelings, and purposes) and the inmost hearts (Rev. 2:23, Amp.).

It is time we moved up. Our hearts are calling us to something more powerful and fulfilling than what has become the normal Christian experience.

The obvious question is, "How do we break this cycle of the hireling church?" It must be done and I believe this is the hour. But although we have gotten ourselves into this mess, I don't believe God will leave us to get ourselves out. God is intervening. In this chapter you'll learn about two biblical ways the church is being confronted—by God's swinging plumb bob and by angels.

GOD'S PLUMB BOB

Edom was a nation that tormented Israel. Isaiah prophesied that God would stretch out upon Edom the "line of confusion, and the stones of emptiness" (Is. 34:11, KJV).

The phrase "stones of emptiness" is peculiar to this verse. You don't find this phrase anywhere else. The Amplified translates the phrase "the plummet stones of chaos."

It refers to a stone mason's plummet, which is a string with a weight of some kind on the end. Today we'd call it a plumb bob. The ancient stone mason used his plummet to see whether a wall was set straight on its foundation or leaned to one direction.

The idea was that God would drop a plumb bob from heaven and take a good look at Edom, which had caused so many problems for Zion. And when He saw that they didn't measure up and were not on the proper foundation, He would swing the plumb bob. As He swayed it, everything that was built incorrectly would be destroyed. The plumb bob would be empowered to knock it down and utterly lay it to waste.

This is an excellent example of how God is moving in His church. He is sending His Spirit to speak and convict both the ministry and the congregation, and if they don't repent and get back on the correct foundation, then that Spirit is empowered to bring them down.

I believe the hour has come when only those who truly humble themselves, seek His face (not His hand), and turn from their ways to His are going to see great revival. If we mix our ways into the wall it's going to lean and fall. The plumb bob has already begun to swing. It has hit those who have lifted themselves highest first. But it is being lowered and those who may not have household names will be next.

But as God knocks down every high thing that exalts itself, whether it be employment of secular thinking or wayward organizations, He doesn't do it as punishment. I believe He does it out of His grace. He so loves you and I He doesn't want us following this example but wants us to build on better foundations.

God's desire is that we lean on Him rather than build something that leans. Oh how rich is the mercy that breaks down every false idol till we see Him! He wants to reveal Himself.

When Simon has that wonderful revelation that Jesus is the Son of God, Jesus responded, "And upon this rock I will build my church" (Matt. 16:18, KJV).

He didn't say that you or I, or anyone else for that matter, would build the church. He said He would. That being the case, I must let Him build. I must stay out of the way and simply do what I am asked. Anything I or anyone else builds, no matter how large the organization or its reputation, is not the church—at least not His church.

Jesus is knocking every false church down. Out of His wonderful mercy for us comes the plumb bob of chaos. He wishes to reveal to us that anything He doesn't build, no matter how it may appear to our senses, is emptiness and chaos.

ANGELS OF DELIVERANCE

All through Scripture God sends powerful deliverance. Some deliverances are more frightening than a heavenly plumb bob, especially deliverance at the hand of an angel. Every time we see an angel, the first thing the angel says is, "Fear not."

Check out the description of cherubim in Ezekiel 1. They looked like men but had four faces—the face of a man in front, a lion on the right side, an ox on the left and an eagle on the back. Their legs were straight and their feet were like that of a calf. They sparkled like burnished bronze. They had the hands of men under their four wings. And hot coals and lightning shot from their bodies (Ezek. 1:5–14).

The seraphim, another rank of angel, has six wings. Isaiah said two wings stretched outward and upward in praise with two wings they covered themselves in humility and with two they flew about in obedience (Is. 6:2–6).

Now that sounds like Stephen Spielberg, Jurassic Park, scary stuff. Yet the Word says God sends angels like these for deliverance. Let's look at some assignments God has given angels.

Jacob met a wrestling angel in Genesis 32:22–32. Maybe God will send an angel to wrestle control of the church from preachers and boards. Some churches would be fine if they weren't "deacon-possessed."

An angel of fire that doesn't consume met Moses (Ex. 3:2). We definitely need a new fire and compassion that doesn't destroy those around us but transmits revelation and direction.

Balaam met an adversarial angel (Num. 22:22). It was sent to stop him from disobedience. The Lord knows in this rebellious and self-serving hour we need the Lord to send an angel to stop us.

There's a "shut-up" angel in Daniel 6:22. He shut the mouths of lions. Of all the angels, this may be the one we need most. This angel steps in when we go to talk about ourselves and what we've accomplished and shuts us up. He shuts up gossip, slander, griping, complaining, cursing, discouraging whispers and faultfinding. What church wouldn't benefit from that angel!

But whatever the angel may be that's needed, God has one.

Paul notes:

> For there stood by me this night the angel of God, whose I am, and whom I serve.
> —Acts 27:23, KJV

Paul had a standby angel. He just stood by, ready to move at God's command to meet the need.

Even though today's church seems to be imprisoned and asleep, God's angels will strike us and wake us as one did to Peter in Acts 12:7. God wants us awake to the problem.

But I believe that God is waiting on a response from us. There are some things God will not do, not even by the hand of angels.

Simon Peter was in jail asleep between two soldiers fastened with two chains. An angel of the Lord appeared beside him and struck him on his side wakening him (Acts 12). He was leading Peter out to freedom.

Simon might have wondered about how they would get past the guards, the chains, the prison doors, the guardrooms and all the people on the streets without causing an alarm. But none of that was a problem for miraculous deliverance.

Even with such miraculous power in operation, the angel instructed Peter to dress himself. There are some things God leaves to the individual. God will shake us awake, but there are some things He is expecting you and I to attend to in order to complete the desired work.

RESPOND TO THE CALL

The plumb bob of God is swinging. The angels have been dispatched. Wake up, church! The ministry of the hireling must cease. It's OK to come into the kingdom as a hireling, but it's a problem when you remain one.

If we continue as hirelings, every bit of peace and joy we receive at salvation is short lived. Many hirelings in fact backslide entirely because sin is pleasant and gratifying for a season—more gratifying than being a hireling.

Hirelings focus on working for a reward, but the rewards of God are found in the depths of relationship, not the work of the kingdom. For us to find satisfaction, our work must issue out of relationship. If our relationship is being based on our works, then carnal gratification and payday will keep us in a hireling mode.

Hear me, church! Wake up! We must be delivered. No amount of success, recognition or physical reward will ever give you peace beyond your understanding. It will all leave you empty, hollow, cold and comfortless.

But when you do what you do because you love

Him rather than to get a payday you will never be left empty, hollow or comfortless. No prison bars can be forged from love. It is freedom. It is joy unspeakable and full of glory.

Lay this book down. Repent for your remaining a hireling. It is time to step up and into Him.

There are times to take a look at ourselves. Careful examination will lead to repentance. This is why the church has an altar. To be honest with you, I never trust anyone who I've never seen go to the altar during altar call. If the preaching is some kind of sloppy emotionalism or "touchy-feely John and his buddies going fishing" sermon without any call for commitment, that is one thing. No one will sense the drawing of the Holy Spirit in this case.

But if the Word of God is preached with the conviction of the Holy Spirit, everyone should feel the challenge. And some time or other everyone should get under conviction. After all, God knows exactly who we are and where we are going. Any person who can sit service after service without any conviction falling does not want Jesus. And if conviction falls and they make excuses without responding to the altar, then they are eaten up with pride.

We must stay tender. Talk to us, Holy Ghost. What are we hiding from ourselves?

Chapter 8

Growing Into Servanthood

IF THE HIRELING represents our relationship with the Lord in its infancy and childhood, then it stands to reason there are scriptural steps for growth. After we repent for being stuck in hireling mode, we can move to the next scriptural step up. We can find it in the very first phrase of John 15:15: "I no longer call you servants . . ." (NIV).

For a long time the disciples were part of the crowd that followed Jesus. Although they had been chosen and were pulled aside by Him, they often thought just like the rest of the crowd. But there came a defining moment, a moment where they had to make a choice.

It was an unnatural choice Jesus was looking for, a faith step, a point where they abandoned the obvious reality and grasped the impossible. That defining moment is described in John 6.

Jesus had walked across the Sea of Galilee to join

His disciples who were rowing a boat to the other side. A large crowd found Jesus and His disciples on shore. They were amazed to see Jesus because they knew He had not been in the disciples' boat when it left shore. Jesus knew their hearts and responded:

> I assure you, most solemnly I tell you, you have been searching for Me, not because you saw the miracles and signs but because you were fed with the loaves and were filled and satisfied.
>
> Stop toiling and doing and producing for the food that perishes and decomposes [in the using], but strive and work and produce rather for the [lasting] food which endures [continually] unto life eternal; the Son of Man will give (furnish) you that, for God the Father has authorized and certified Him and put His seal of endorsement upon Him.
>
> —JOHN 6:26–27, AMP.

They still didn't grasp that He was calling upon them to take a step beyond merely believing God for that which satisfies the carnal senses.

Instead of stepping up to faith, they demanded Jesus to give them a sign that He was worth their continued allegiance. That's a hireling attitude if I ever saw one. "Give us and we will do what you have paid us to do." No pay. No allegiance.

In fact, they clamored for more manna. Free bread was their motive. Free bread was their goal.

Jesus spent almost twenty verses discussing the issue before He seemed to tire of the conversation. Finally He just blew them out of the water. He told them that He is the bread.

I can just imagine their bug-eyed reaction to His comment. Then when He went on to tell them they must eat His flesh and drink His blood it just blew their minds. It was probably a very small explosion. Hardly any smoke, I'll wager.

But to these pious, religious folks, Jesus was speaking blasphemy and confusion. But what they didn't understand was that He had stepped up to another level and was talking down to them. It was a challenge to come up higher. But most of them couldn't grasp these new wondrous possibilities. The crowd immediately gave Him relief of responsibilities for their souls. They all left.

But the disciples stayed. When asked if they would also go they simply said, "Where shall we go? You have the words of life." They didn't understand what He meant either, but they had been with Him long enough to know what He didn't mean.

This is the challenge. Will you leave the relationship level that is personally satisfying and easily understandable and step up to the level of personal loyalty and obedience, whether you understand the whys and wherefores or not?

Jesus says to us, "Will you eat My flesh and drink My blood?" If not, you will find any other satisfaction to be fleeting and temporary.

New Manna

Perhaps the crowd did not understand what Jesus meant when He said He would be their bread. But the Book of Revelation clarifies His words for us today. Revelation 2:17 says to those who overcome He will give to eat of the hidden manna and He will give them a new name of relationship that no one else knows.

Now the only place manna was ever hidden was the ark of the covenant. The manna was in there with Aaron's rod that budded and the two tablets of the commandments. The Ark was the symbol of the God's presence, leadership, authority and blessing. It was topped by two angels watching over the mercy set. It was the visible symbol of God's covenant of deliverance and provision. It included everything from manna to mercy.

Jesus was saying to these Jews that He was the new ark of the new covenant. In Him was the rod of spiritual authority. In Him was the Word with its commands and promises. In Him was the manna, the spiritual food for all.

Jesus is our ark of the covenant. Some wonderful visual symbols confirm this. For example, when Mary looked into Jesus' empty tomb, she saw two angels sitting inside, one on each end of the slab where Jesus had lain (John 20:12). He is our mercy seat. Notice the angels were sitting, not standing up guarding as they were on the Old Testament ark. Historically, cherubim are always standing in service with raised wings. But now the work is finished. Mercy there is great, and is free—free to all who accept it. But this step of acceptance is one we must choose to make.

I have already been bought and paid for. Jesus doesn't owe me anything. If He never answered another prayer or ever spoke to me again I have already received far beyond what I deserve. I will never expect a payday. I'm already paid for. I am His! I can't stay in the hireling mentality.

The crowd in John 6 couldn't understand the manna of the new covenant. But the disciples stepped up at this point from hirelings to servants. They decided they didn't need to understand. They chose to trust Him.

But there is still plenty of room for you and I. The kingdom is very large. The invitation is for us also. We can move up. In fact, He expects us to do so.

GIVING UP RIGHTS

We are His workmanship, says Ephesians 2:10. Now the Amplified says "handiwork," but the thought is much the same. The Greek word is *poiema*, from which we get our word *poem*. It simply means that God has already written the epic poem, or ode of the ages, and you and I are already in it.

Many Jews believe that everything we do in the will of God simply matches what He has already written for us. Isn't that powerful? We are already in God's history of the church. He made room in His poem for you.

It's time to step in and pick up our part. But it's the only thing you're allowed to have. You lose ownership of everything else. You lose your rights. Everything becomes His. The only thing you are left with is responsibility and full acceptance. You are responsible for every task He assigns you, and He fully accepts you.

Jesus owns my house, bank account, car, family, church and everything else. Everything that had been mine becomes His because He bought me. This includes my bills, my relationships (both good and bad), my marriage, even my health. But it's all right. He knew that before He bought me.

But giving up ownership and rights is very, very difficult for some. Jesus ran into these problems among some who wanted to follow Him, especially a young man we've come to refer to as the rich young ruler (Matt. 19:16–28).

Here is a young man who lived, by his own testimony, a holy life. Jesus didn't contradict this statement or even correct him for self-righteousness. This young man seems to have been truly hungry to obey the Lord.

But there is a problem. At first it may seem to be greed, but his problem was actually fear. He was trusting in his money. It wasn't that he didn't love Jesus. But self-preservation took authority.

Insecurity concerning the future held him in a death grip. He could not bear the thought of losing control of his future. He had already made the decision to serve God, and the thought of turning back hadn't entered his mind. But the cost of moving forward kept him immobile.

Whenever God powerfully speaks to me to do something, if I look at the circumstances I hesitate. It never looks like what would be best for me in the long run.

Every time God has told me to change pastorates it has been to a smaller church with less money. Now these always grew and in the end I would be better off than at the previous church. But it still looked like a dumb move at that moment.

At times I have even had dear friends call me and say, "Pat, don't do this. It will be the end of your ministry and career when you go there. No one will ever hear from you again."

But I always respond that I don't have a career. I have a relationship. Jesus didn't call me to preach or to pastor. He called me to Him and then assigned me some duties on the way.

OWNED BY MINISTRY?

Many preachers have what I call "water faucet and light fixture" ministries. Let me explain with an illustration.

Sometimes my wife goes to bed before me. She loves to lay and read. As for me, when I lay down, something in my head says it's time to go to sleep. So if I'm going to read I must sit up in a chair. Now when my wife hears my recliner pull up she knows I'm on my way. Since I come through the kitchen on my way to our room she will sometimes ask me to bring her a glass of water.

Suppose I go to the kitchen for that water and when I open the cabinet I become captivated by the variety of glasses—short ones, tall ones, little ones, big ones of every shape and color. I count how many we have, and then I count how many we have of each sort. I rejoice in how full I can fill each one. I look at how much it will hold and how long it takes to get one filled. I spend time rearranging them and seeing how many I can get on each pew, excuse me, I mean shelf.

I then notice the water faucet. How lovely and exquisite it is. I adjust the flow until it's in order and doesn't splash. I see how much control I have of the flow and whether it can be mixed with enough warm to keep the chill out but certainly not hot enough to burn.

You would say, "What kind of fool are you?" And I would quickly agree. The one I love is in the bedroom. The water is for her. I have just been asked to carry water on my way, not fall in love with how I get it.

It's so easy to forget the purpose behind what we do. Have you noticed how some people love the light? They notice that the brighter it is, the clearer everything is. So they study electricity and dissect light bulbs until they have more information than the average. They can talk light fixtures. They can assess proper pronunciation of Greek and Hebrew appliances. Unfortunately, they sometimes get so close to hot lights they burn out themselves. It's simply due to the fact they have forgotten what it was they wanted to see clearly.

We weren't saved so we could study and gain knowledge about Him, nor fall in love with ministry or its provisions. He called us to Him. He died that we might know Him.

The rich young ruler couldn't let go. His possessions possessed Him. Many Christians are owned by their ministry. It controls their security, their future, their livelihood and even their personalities. They no longer are capable of letting go, so they cannot move forward in Jesus, only in the ministry.

One thing I thought was amazing about this story is what Jesus said to the rich ruler in the twenty-first verse:

> If thou wilt be perfect, go and sell that thou hast, and give to the poor, and thou shalt have treasure in heaven: and come and follow me.
>
> —MATTHEW 19:21, KJV

Obviously this young man didn't grasp the power of this—the King of heaven offering the treasury. But even more significantly the only other people Jesus told "follow Me" were the disciples. Could it be that this was the man Jesus had chosen to replace Judas? (Ironically, Judas was also possessed by the earthly treasury.)

In addition, if this man had stuck around for the rest of the sermon, he would have heard something very captivating. After Jesus stated how hard it is for a rich man to get into heaven, Simon spoke up:

> Behold, we have forsaken all, and followed thee; what shall we have therefore?
>
> —MATTHEW 19:27, KJV

Jesus responded:

> Truly I say to you, in the new age (the Messianic rebirth of the world), when the Son of Man shall sit down on the throne of His glory, you who have [become My disciples, sided with My party and] followed Me will also sit in twelve thrones and judge the twelve tribes of Israel. And anyone and everyone who has left houses or brothers or sisters or father or mother or children or lands for My name's sake will receive many [even a hundred] times more and will inherit eternal life.
>
> —MATTHEW 19:28–29, AMP.

Luke adds, "Who will not receive in return many times more in this world and, in the coming age, eternal life" (Luke 18:30). Jesus was talking in terms of investment. Give Me your life now, and when My kingdom comes I will give you a much better life in return. The rich ruler should have understood investing. But when it appeared as though he would lose what he had, then he went back to the life of pseudo-religion, where he had more control and security.

Saints, let go. Do what Jesus asks. As long as you

have things and rights you're obligated to protect them. Jesus made himself of no reputation so He never had to protect even that. Give it up. Surrender! Get down in your spirit and stir up the Jesus in you. He is the Author and Finisher of our faith. Let Him authorize you a little more. Then step out into what He's telling you.

I can hear, "Sure, Pat, but what if I fail?"

I'll tell you quickly. Without Him you're a failure anyway. You have nothing to lose. Be a servant.

Chapter 9

Servants Have Unity

THE SECOND POINT of biblical order from Genesis 1:1 now comes into play. Remember that the first point of order is relationship. The second is unity. In fact, I personally believe that unity is the strongest teaching in the Word from Genesis to Revelation, and the strongest teaching of the Jewish believers also. In this chapter you will learn how servanthood will bring the church into biblical order in the area of unity.

CLIQUES AND SPIRITS

Paul had heard a rumor about the unity in the church at Corinth.

> For in the first place, when you assemble as a congregation, I hear that there are cliques (divisions and factions) among you; and I in part believe it.
>
> —1 CORINTHIANS 11:18, AMP.

Today the one thing no one doubts about the church is the ability for there to be cliques and splits. They are everywhere. Disunity is an aspect of the hireling mentality that is mended by a servant relationship. When you are a servant and give up rights, ownership and reputation then you no longer have to look at anyone else as a threat. There is nothing to fear. They cannot take anything you haven't already given up. Paul says wryly that the good side of these cliques is that they identify the genuine saint from the heretic (1 Cor. 11:19, KJV).

Webster defines a *heretic* as "a church member who holds a belief opposed to church dogma." Because unity is a point of biblical order, those who bring disruption and strife are heretics.

Unity is based on the vision of the church. There must be one solid vision focused on by all. This vision isn't to come up from the congregation but down from the Lord. He is the one who gave the church the five-fold ministry as a gift. The vision must come through the God-assigned leadership, though. God may confirm the vision to members of the congregation. If any other vision arises, it isn't God.

The prefix meaning two is *di*, which is how we get the word *division*. More than one vision is **di**vision. This isn't God. A house divided against itself cannot stand (Luke 11:17). It is impossible. Jesus said it and that's as powerful an authority as you will find.

Let me give you another example of the need and power of unity. When God looked down upon the people of Babel, He said:

> Behold, they are one people and they have
> all one language; and this is only the begin-

ning of what they will do, and now nothing
they have imagined they can do will be
impossible for them.

—GENESIS 11:6, AMP.

Did it strike you like it did me? God said they were
in unity and anything they could imagine was possible
for them. What unbelievable power for heathens—
not Holy-Ghost-filled Christians—but unbelieving
heathens. And God said it. Not anyone else but God
Himself. That is pretty good authority. Unfortunately,
most of the churches of today are in such disunity they
don't have the power to blow their own nose.

I believe the whole purpose of the infilling of the
Spirit (Acts 2:4) is that we become one people, of one
language and operating in the unity that turns hell
inside out. Acts 17:26 says we are one blood. But by
the Spirit of God we are also one spirit, one people
with one God, one focus and one purpose.

Jesus made unity one of His most often mentioned
subjects. In fact, just count the references to unity in
John 17. This is the one prayer Jesus let us know He
prayed for us as His church.

> And [now] I am no more in the world, but
> these are [still] in the world, and I am
> coming to You. Holy Father, keep in Your
> Name [in the knowledge of Yourself] those
> whom You have given Me, that they may be
> one as We [are one].
>
> —JOHN 17:11, AMP.

And again later in the same prayer,

That they all may be one, [just] as You, Father, are in Me and I in You, that they also may be one in Us, so that the world may believe and be convinced that You have sent Me. I have given to them the glory and honor which You have given Me, that they may be one [even] as We are one: I in them and You in Me, in order that they may become one and perfectly united, that the world may know and [definitely] recognize that You sent Me and that You have loved them [even] as You have loved Me.

—JOHN 17:21-23, AMP.

Jesus says in His prayer that the world will believe on Him because of our unity. To empower us to that end, we have received His prayer, glory and honor. All of this that we may be one. And yet the church is anything but one. Talk about missing God. But when as a servant you lose rights, ownership and reputation, it is possible to become the answer to Jesus' prayer.

In most cases it isn't the world that is causing the church's disunity. Instead, when the church is persecuted it becomes powerful because the people stayed focused on their faith for survival.

A missionary to the former Soviet Union told me that before the fall of communism, the church behind the iron curtain was powerful. There was no sectarian thought. The church was growing, and miracles were prevalent no matter what the theological stand. Pentecostals, Nazarenes, Presbyterians and Baptists all had fellowship. But when the iron curtain fell, disunity became rampant. Sectarianism took over. It is now dog eat dog with total chaos and no cooperation.

Few are being saved and the miracles have all but ceased. It is only outside the organized church anything good is happening. Does that sound familiar?

Pastors against pastors. Pastors protecting churches from boards and boards protecting churches from pastors. Saint verses saint is the venue of nearly every situation where nothing supernaturally powerful is taking place.

If we don't move towards unity we try formulas, talent, music, polished pulpiteers and every other pleasant-to-the-senses replacement. But none of these changes lives. Jesus knew this certainly, and that's why He spent time telling us to avoid the pitfall. This is why it is the one and only prayer recorded that was specifically prayed by Jesus for us.

RESTORING UNITY

It is time we paid attention to what the Bible says about relationship and unity. Jesus more or less states that unity and relationship are more important than giving (Matt. 5:23). Boy, that thought is contrary to the pulpit message of many churches! Before you give, Jesus says to get things right with your brother.

Jesus said that if you have a disagreement with someone and he begins to make accusations, you are to come to agreement with him as quickly as possible.

Come to terms quickly with your accuser while you are on the way traveling with him, lest your accuser hand you over to the judge, and the judge to the guard, and you be put in prison (Matt. 5:25, Amp.).

Did you catch the thought, "While you are on the way traveling with him?" This isn't referring to some sinner outside the church. Every commentary I have

read agrees that this verse is speaking of those in the
way of the Lord, those who are in the church with us.
And if we don't come to agreement with them, there
are dire results. Our accuser will turn us over to the
judge. Or it could be said that he will pray and the
Judge of us all will hear. Until the matter is resolved,
we are locked up.

Today people come in to our churches sick, unhappy,
sinful and empty. They often leave the same way. Could
it be that our blessings and power are locked up?

Verse 26 says we will remain locked up till the problem
is solved. That's why Satan is an accuser. He keeps us
locked up by simply turning us against each other.

Our relationships are so important because God
places great value on every believer. Jesus told a
parable about a good shepherd who left ninety-nine
sheep to retrieve the one who had "gone astray." We
can tell that Jesus was speaking of those gone astray
due to disunity among believers because His very next
teaching was on how to reconcile an offense between
Christian brothers.

> If your brother wrongs you, go and show
> him his fault, between you and him privately.
> If he listens to you, you have won back your
> brother. But if he does not listen, take along
> with you one or two others, so that every
> word may be confirmed and upheld by the
> testimony of two or three witnesses.
> —MATTHEW 18:15–16, AMP.

This is just the beginning of several clear and con-
cise steps for dealing with relationship problems. If all
attempts fail, Jesus explains the consequences for the

offending party. The Bible says that once the injured party and those he has brought the situation before agree together concerning the impropriety and unrighteousness of the action, then heaven agrees with anything you declare lawful or unlawful. Then comes a reiteration of the teaching.

Again I tell you, if two of you on earth agree (harmonize together, make a symphony together) about whatever [anything and everything] they may ask, it will come to pass and be done for them by My Father in heaven. For wherever two or three are gathered (drawn together as My followers) in (into) My name, there I AM in the midst of them [Exod. 3:14] (Matt. 18:19–20, Amp.).

When Jesus is talking about two people agreeing, is He talking about just any two who call themselves Christians and go to church? No, He speaks of those who are drawn to focus in Him. I've been lots of places where there were two Christians, but there wasn't any sense of supernatural power or presence at all.

It is two or more coming together for Him and in Him. This is their purpose and His presence is their goal. But again, the power of coming together as Christians is part of the larger teaching of dealing with relationship problems.

Simon Peter recognized that relationship was Jesus' theme, and so he asked:

Lord, how many times may my brother sin against me and I forgive him and let it go? [As many as] up to seven times?
—MATTHEW 18:21, AMP.

Jesus made the familiar and famous reply—seventy

times seven—then went on teaching about the kingdom and the king settling accounts with his subjector. The parable ends by warning that if we don't forgive our brother, the Lord will punish us.

Keeping Peace

If you study Jewish teaching on relationship you will find it to be central to all they believe. In fact, many Jewish scholars believe God allowed Jerusalem to be destroyed by Rome because of the Jews' unrighteous hatred toward other people.

When you read the Book of Hebrews, a book written by a Jew to Jews, you see the relationship emphasis again.

Follow peace with all men, and holiness, without which no man shall see the Lord (Heb. 12:14, KJV).

We Americans tend to emphasize the holiness thought. But the holiness is the afterthought. It is peace that is really being emphasized, "without which no man shall see the Lord." Of course, following peace with all men shouldn't be a problem since we are to have so much peace that it passes human understanding.

The importance God places on being at peace with others is backed by several other passages.

It if be possible, as much lieth in you, live peaceably with all men.
—Romans 12:18, KJV

Let us therefore follow after the things which make for peace, and things wherewith one may edify another.
—Romans 14:19, KJV

Now I beseech you, brethren, by the name of our Lord Jesus Christ, that ye all speak the same thing, and that there be no divisions among you; but that ye be perfectly joined together in the same mind and in the same judgment.

—1 CORINTHIANS 1:10, KJV

But the wisdom that is from above is first pure, then peaceable, gentle, and easy to be entreated, full of mercy and good fruits, without partiality, and without hypocrisy. And the fruit of righteousness is sown in peace of them that make peace.

—JAMES 3:17–18, KJV

I hope you're convinced, but this study of peace is by no means exhaustive. The list can go on and on because being at peace with one another is a priority with God.

Unity is absolutely essential. In fact, even the kabala, the most mystic of all Jewish literature, is built on the premise of unity. Without unity there is no such thing as a church or the body of Christ. We are impotent, dead and without spiritual significance.

But unity only comes when we surrender our rights and choose to follow Jesus' agenda, person and presence. As long as we are after anything else, we must fight and wrestle and deal with jealousy and competition. But as servants protecting our rights isn't necessary. All that is important is decided and protected by Jesus Himself. All we have to do is trust the Master.

Chapter 10

A Servant's Expectations

GOING FROM HIRELING to servant has a major effect on your day-to-day living. It wasn't until the disciples stepped up into servanthood that Jesus sent them out two by two and they discovered that they possessed the same power over demons and sickness that Jesus had. The more we surrender and trust Jesus, the more He is able to entrust us with supernatural authority. When we become servants of His then His authority becomes ours. We know we only have that authority in His name, so there is no danger of us using Him or His authority to our personal advantage. But along with power and authority comes a greater responsibility.

Responsibility is a major factor of relationship. Any time you have trust, the person entrusted has the responsibility of living up to that trust. This chapter tells what a servant is responsible to do, but it also

A Servant's Expectations

addresses the confusion servants feel when God doesn't respond according to their expectations.

OBEDIENCE

When Moses was about to turn the reins of leadership over to Joshua, he was given instructions from the Lord.

> The Lord said to Moses, Take Joshua son of Nun, a man in whom is the Spirit, and lay your hand upon him.
> —NUMBERS 27:18, AMP.

God told Moses to lay "his hand" on Joshua, but verse 23 says Moses laid both hands on him. Moses knew the weight of responsibility he passed on to Joshua. Contrary to what some believe, a leader's major responsibility is not caring for people—wiping noses and solving the disputes of neighbors over their children. Not at all! A leader has the responsibility of hearing from God and leading the people through hostile territory. But the ultimate goal is to lead others to Jesus and bring them to maturity and victory in Christ. We are our brother's keeper, but not our brother's nursemaid.

I'm not talking about being there in crisis or emergency, or even guiding by advice. But I am talking about a church keeping the pastor so busy waiting tables that he has no time for prayer and study.

By the way, winning the lost is for everyone, not just the pastor. We are not to hold the fort; we are to storm the gates. Once you have become a real servant you can do nothing but become radically obedient to His every whisper.

99

The mind-set has changed from getting to giving. The whole of life is ready to be spent to know Him. Worship becomes *to* Him rather than *at* Him or even *for* Him. Even the motive for living a holy and modest lifestyle changes. A holy life becomes a means of worship rather than a way to stay saved. Even your prayer time becomes an experience of intimacy that leads to service.

EXPECTATIONS

Jesus described the servant's lifestyle to His disciples in Luke 17:7–10:

> Will any man of you who has a servant plowing or tending sheep say to him when he has come in from the field, Come at once and take your place at the table?
>
> Will he not instead tell him, Get my supper ready and gird yourself and serve me while I eat and drink; then afterward you yourself shall eat and drink?
>
> Is he grateful and does he praise the servant because he did what he was ordered to do?
>
> Even so on your part, when you have done everything that was assigned and commanded you, say, We are unworthy servants [possessing no merit, for we have not gone beyond our obligation]; we have [merely] done what was our duty to do (Amp.).

Jesus says the servant is responsible to obey and shouldn't count his obedience as some extraordinary service to receive great reward. By obeying, we as servants are only doing our duty. Since we are bought and paid for we now are to spend our lives for Him. But in return for spending our lives in obedience, we share of the master's provisions. We dwell in His presence. We operate in—as well as under—His authority. But even in the servant relationship there can be pitfalls. Sometimes familiarity with the Lord can result in a certain self-righteousness and a sense that He should do a little more for you than others. Also as you're operating in obedience sometimes things don't happen as you expect them to. One time He heals and the next time He doesn't. At other times you receive instructions and so you do A and B as you were told, but instead of coming up with the expected C result you get a Z or P or W. Since you don't grasp any order to what you're doing and what the results should be, it is easy to become frustrated.

Let me give you an example. Let's look at Jesus in John 11. After some delays Jesus finally arrived in Bethany as summoned by Mary and Martha, but, as you know, Lazarus had died in the meantime. When Martha heard Jesus was coming she went to meet Him (v. 20). This is a little strange. Jewish customs required she stay at home and mourn her brother for at least seven days after his death. Other than to attend the funeral and burial she must remain indoors. Even today if a Jew is in the week of mourning they put sand in their shoes if they go out for an emergency reminding them with every step that they must quickly take care of the emergency and then return home.

Mourning is an important and solemn time. For as long as a year, the next-of-kin may even sit on a chair or on a stool shorter than any other seat in the home. This is to be a reminder that life will never look the same since their loved ones have left it.

But Martha went out and met Jesus. She was upset yet sure that Jesus could at least help her pain if nothing else. Though Martha reached out to Jesus, Mary remained at home. Why would Mary stay home if Martha went out?

This is Mary, the one who sat at Jesus' feet. Mary, the one who anointed Jesus' feet for burial and dried them with her tears. Mary, who so loved Jesus yet now is self-righteously pouting because Jesus didn't come when He was summoned. He didn't do what she wanted when she wanted. So she stayed at home.

When Jesus did get to the tomb and demanded it to be opened, the two sisters told Him that Lazarus stunk. But the stench won't stop Him from moving in and performing a miracle. Jesus has always been ready to move into the stinking messes of our lives and bring His resurrection power. But when Mary doesn't come out to meet Him, He stops. He waits, unwilling to move. Could it be that the stench of her self-righteous perturbed pouting was worse than the smell of Lazarus' decaying flesh?

Jesus stayed where He met Martha till Mary came. When Mary heard from Martha that Jesus had asked for her, she jumped up and ran immediately to Him. She realized that He had not forgotten her after all. He was just operating differently than she expected, and she had become frustrated not knowing what He was really doing.

Jesus said in John 15:15, "The servant does not know what his master is doing (working out)" (Amp.). In that statement is the answer to a great deal of servant frustration. Jesus has often told me to do things, yet as many times as not, the outcome of my obedience was not what I expected.

I have at times taken stands that were unpopular. In each situation I had prayed, sought God and fasted before I took my stand. I knew what I was to do. Yet the result was anger and hard times from the church people. They didn't or couldn't agree with me. Sometimes they even got so angry they became physical. Twice I have been physically struck even though I had heard from God and was standing firm on biblical principles. In each case I was only struck once, and although the Detroit rose up in me real quick I didn't return the blow. God gave me grace. But I couldn't understand. I became frustrated and, although I wouldn't quickly admit it, I got angry with God. How could He let them do this to me? In church, no less.

For years the frustration built up, especially when God sent me to a church that no one wanted to pastor. I thought if I prayed and listened and preached truth and worked hard, then the church would have to explode in growth. I prayed, preached, worked and did all the right things but was constantly under attack from those already attending. Now I don't mean to say that no one stood with me or that nothing positive happened. There were always good people, and every church did grow. But not the way I expected.

You see, I was expecting a certain result—the one that I thought was reasonable and good for the kingdom. I didn't grasp that God was trying to do something else entirely. As a result, when God told me to leave the church, I went away thinking I was a failure because what I thought should happen hadn't. I hadn't learned the lesson that I couldn't fail Him except by being disobedient. Since I had obeyed everything I knew He said, I was a success, not a failure.

Someone might say, "Pat, you might not have heard everything."

Well, I suppose that is possible but not probable. I can't find it anywhere in the Bible where it says find the will of God. I only find where it says obey the will of God. The issue isn't whether or not I'm big enough to hear what He says. The issue is whether or not God is big enough to speak loudly enough for me to hear.

Let me explain how God speaks. Saul was on his way to Damascus on what he believed was a holy quest, a mission from God, to kill as many of those heretic Christians as possible. God hit him with lightning, knocked him to the ground and blinded him to everything else around him. Then God said, "I am Jesus whom thou persecutest: it is hard for thee to kick against the pricks [or ox goad]" (Acts 9:5, KJV). The ox goad was designed to steer the ox in a desired direction. If the ox kicked against it, it hurt! God says it is very, very difficult for a person to miss the will of God when they want the will of God. In other words, God's direction will be detectable, to say the least. Saul really wanted the will of God, so God took drastic measures to speak to Him. God will do whatever it takes to stop you if you think you are doing His will, but you're not. He is a very big God.

One time I went to prayer seeking God for wisdom concerning how to lead the church. I told Him that I was afraid I would miss Him and that revival in the church and in our city would be forfeited. I waited patiently for an answer and then finally I could swear I heard God chuckle. That's right, I said chuckle. Then

I heard that still, small voice of peace whisper to me, "Don't worry, Pat. You're not big enough to stop Me!"

The servant who doesn't grasp the reality of God's ability will continue in feelings of great frustration. The emotional turmoil may even mix with anger. A root of bitterness may eventually take hold and begin to affect the servant's vision and performance. Never forget that the prayer that moves a saint from one level of relationship to another is always a prayer of surrender.

We say, "Whatever it takes Lord to make me be what You want me to be, do it, Lord. I give myself to You." But then when it begins to happen we are so caught up in our own logic we grow weary of situations and results that we can't understand. It is time to step up again. There is still one higher level of relationship found in the Word.

There is a greater truth than human logic. It is this kind of truth that makes me free. It is the truth of moving and growing up in Jesus. It makes everything I do for Jesus worthwhile, no matter what I must personally endure. The Jews believe that these powerful truths only come to you and stay with you when they are accompanied by suffering. Well, everything I have learned has been that way. I paid and continue to pay my dues. But it is accompanied by real, living and vital revelation.

The Jewish people believe that in the end all those in hell will have to praise God when they see how terrible sin is and its punishment. From hell they will have learned what a great and merciful God is and will praise His eternal judgments, even the ones that resulted in their being in hell. The New Testament expresses this belief as well.

That in (at) the name of Jesus every knee should (must) bow, in heaven and on earth and under the earth. And every tongue [frankly and openly] confess *and* acknowledge that Jesus Christ is Lord, to the glory of God the Father.
—PHILIPPIANS 2:10–11, AMP., ITALICS ADDED

SUMMARY

Expectations of God's performance based on human logic will lead to frustration and even bitterness. While a servant works hard for God, he must remember that God is under no obligation to perform according to the servant's idea of what is best. A servant will learn from experience that God's plan is best—even if it involves suffering along the way!

Chapter 11

A Servant's Level of Authority

I AM A WORKAHOLIC. It is a sin, and I confess it as such. I try to tell my wife that there is something worse than a workaholic. That is a person who is allergic to work. But it is hard for me to find a balance in my lifestyle because I really *like* to spend hours studying and reading.

Servants often become workaholics and rarely take time to truly rest and relax. But they also believe God wants them to find something enjoyable, therefore, many ministers (like myself) fall in love with the Word and revelation. It becomes our way to have fun and stay "above average" in the ministry. When we were hirelings, pleasing people was the hook. It was the one thing that gave us a feeling of security and pleasure. But as servants, if we are not careful, the ministry becomes our hook. We become obsessed with being servants and studying the Word.

It is so wonderful to serve and to be a servant that even

suffering becomes an advantage. You know the Master will bless you for it. My wife says I can get a martyr complex in a Chinese second (that is, "short-lee").

This chapter will tell how servants can overcome their tendency to accept unnecessary pain. It will also show how our shortcomings can give us an opportunity to take a step from servanthood toward friendship.

AUTHORITY

While servants are sincere, steady, hard workers, they have a tendency to overlook their authority in Christ. I've seen this happen in my own life.

I become humbled by God doing things I know I don't deserve, and I find myself being much happier than I deserve to be. This being the case I don't really want to walk in the authority of my position as pastor. It just seems unnecessary to have my own way. Sometimes I can allow my church board or other church leaders to lead in front of me, instead of me leading the church while they follow. It is a fact of life that in a leadership vacuum someone will rise up to lead. If the pastor doesn't take his place, another leader will fill the leadership gap. Never forget that whatever leadership role God has given you is a divine appointment. God isn't confused or foolish. You were the best one for the job, or at least the best that would respond to His call.

All this reminds me of when the ark of the covenant was won in battle by the Philistines. When this trophy of war was placed in their temple, their god Dagon fell on his face during the night. They set him up and the next day he fell again. The nation also became cursed with pestilence, mice and hemorrhoids. They sent the ark back to Israel on a new cart. The Philistines got away with sending the ark back this way because they were heathen (1 Sam. 5–6). When David tried to put the ark on a cart later, it was unacceptable and Uzzah died (2 Sam. 6:1–8).

God will not let His presence be moved by a new cart. After all, a cart is big wheels and boards. That's not how the kingdom is to operate.

But one of the little noticed elements of this story is found when Solomon went to move the ark into the newly constructed temple at its dedication.

> There was nothing in the ark except the two tables [the Ten Commandments] which Moses put in it at Mount Horeb, when the Lord made a covenant with the Israelites when they came out of Egypt.
> —2 CHRONICLES 5:10, AMP.

We are not informed specifically as to what happened to the other two items that had once been contained in the ark—Aaron's rod and a pot of manna (Ex. 16:32–34; Num. 17:8–10). The only time that we know for sure the ark is opened is when it was captured by the Philistines (1 Sam. 4:11). Oral tradition states that God sent the curses upon the Philistines when they opened the ark and removed the rod and the manna. Most scholars believe that the rod and manna were never placed back inside, although there is no traditional statement on whatever became of them.

The missing items from the ark are symbols of what servants often forget. First, they forget their authority, which is represented by Aaron's rod that produced buds, blossoms and ripe almonds. It was a sign that

God had given priestly authority to the house of Levi. Second, servants forget the blessing and provision of God, which is represented by the pot of manna (the food that appeared like dew on the ground as the Israelites wandered the wilderness). Instead, servants tend to focus on the rulings and commands of God, represented by the Ten Commandments, which remained in the ark.

Servants are good at obeying commandments. They have learned that a servant cannot be more or less successful than anyone else, only more obedient. Walking in obedience is good, but authority and blessing come with it. It is a Philistine mentality to try to operate on anything less than all of God. You can't be successful with His authority and provision unless you also obey His commands. By the same token you cannot be successful with obedience alone, either. You must also operate in His authority and provision at the same time.

When we focus exclusively on obedience, we may accept abuse, thinking it is correction for an unknown sin. David reacted this way when he fled from the wicked usurpation of power by his son Absalom. Shimei, from the house of Saul, ridiculed and cursed David, even throwing stones and dust at him. Abishai, the son of Zeruiah, asked David to let him go dispose of the problem, but David responded:

> Behold, my son, who was born to me, seeks my life. With how much more reason now may this Benjamite do it? Let him alone; and let him curse, for the Lord has bidden him to do it.
> —2 Samuel 16:11, Amp.

But then David added a comment that came out of

his knowing the truth that God will avenge the righteous and reward the obedient.

> It may be that the Lord will look on the iniquity done me and will recompense me with good for his cursing this day.
> —2 SAMUEL 16:12, AMP.

Though it was after David's death, Shimei ultimately paid for his actions with his life. (See 1 Kings 2:36–46.) The Lord will avenge even when we do not defend ourselves against false accusations.

There was a time several years ago when I was being ridiculed and people were speaking very unkindly about me. DayStar Assembly of God (the church I pastor) had really begun to grow, but the growth was made up of the undesired and outcast. Drug addicts, prostitutes, pimps, alcoholics and even homosexuals seemed drawn to us. Now, my surrounding pastors could put up with this kind of ministry but not with the added bonus that these people weren't all Anglo-Saxon white.

The church is in Tuscaloosa, Alabama, not New York or Detroit, so the race issue cut both ways. The white pastors said I was trying to be black, and the black pastors said that any black who came to our church was trying to be white.

On top of this, the reputation of the church had been tarnished by immorality before I came to pastor, so they said the church was nurturing a hodge podge of immorality and liberal lifestyles. The pastors who didn't say we were liberal told their people we were some kind of cult because I had a standard of dress for the platform and ministry of the church.

I went to the Lord about these accusations at some length, not because they were valid, but just the opposite. I knew God was doing a great thing. Jesus spoke to my heart and told me not to worry. He said that for every time someone spoke badly about us He would bless me. I believed this to such an extent that when things would slow down I got to hoping I would hear of someone speaking unkindly of us so that I could receive a blessing.

DAVID'S INSIGHT

Sometimes as a servant it will even be friends—those you consider fellow servants—who burn you. Take the case of Ahithophel, for example. Ahithophel was King David's number one counselor. He was so wise that Scripture says his counsel in those days was as if a man had inquired of the oracle of God (2 Sam. 16:23).

But as David's counselor he had ambition of his own. Oral tradition says that it had been prophesied over him that out of his household would spring kings. Now the only problem was that Ahithophel relied on his own wisdom to try to make this happen. He had a niece who lived with him as she grew up. She was married to a Hittite but it wasn't above her uncle to use her as a tool in his scheme. Her name was Bathsheba.

It is believed by many that Ahithophel planned the ceremonial cleansing (bathing) of Bathsheba to be where David would witness it. It seems that Ahithophel thought that by bringing David down he would be exalted. He just wanted to give God that opportunity. After all, he knew all of David's imperfections. He had spent much time with the king, and he knew that God would want to deal with these problems. We know, of course, what came about in the end—Uriah's death, David's marriage to Bathsheba and David's confrontation by the prophet Nathan (2 Sam. 11–12).

But what Ahithophel didn't count on was David's having taken the next step up from servant. Even with his problems David threw himself upon the mercy of God. In front of his courtesans, staff and generals he fell off his throne and threw himself upon the mercy of God. God saw his heart. David's heart was certainly faulty, but deep within it wanted Jehovah. At its core it was chasing the presence of God.

God responded to David's sin in a way He had never responded to sin before. The law written and delivered by God to Moses said that David must die. But God put Himself between David and the law and whispered in David's ear, "Thou shalt not die" (2 Sam. 12:13, KJV).

This is a wonderful and remarkable story to all of us who read it. But to Ahithophel, God's mercy marked an unexpected end to a lofty ambition. So then when Absalom snatched the kingdom from David, Ahithophel went with him. But David planted people to cast doubts to Absalom about Ahithophel's advice. Absalom's rejection was the straw that broke the camel's back. Ahithophel was so humiliated that he went home, set his house in order and committed suicide by hanging (2 Sam. 15–17).

What is truly sad is that the prophecy about kings among Ahithophel's house came true. Remember, Bathsheba was related to Ahithophel, and her second son with David was Solomon, who became king. But anytime a person takes a prophecy and attempts to make it the path of his life, he is a fool and will only meet frustration and failure. A prophecy is given so that a servant may know that if he remains loyal and obedient no matter how things appear or what circumstances seem to work in the opposite direction, the Master will bring the prophecy to pass.

David understood what Ahithophel did not. As servants we must trust it all to the Master. We must be real and honest with ourselves It is best to admit our faults and release our future as servants of the living God. The Lord knows what He is doing. He can be trusted. He obviously knew all that would take place all along. So the prophecy was always accurate.

David had discovered a key. He, in fact, was moving up beyond servant. He was becoming a friend of God. Jesus said to His disciples in John 15:15:

> I do not call you servants (slaves) any longer, for the servant does not know what his master is doing (working out). But I have called you My friends, because I have made known to you everything that I have heard from My Father. [I have revealed to you everything that I have learned from Him] (Amp.).

If you look at that verse closely, you'll see that friendship with God is made possible by what God does for us. Jesus said, "I have called you My friends because I have made known to you everything that I have heard from My Father." He reveals Himself to us so that we can have a friendship relationship with Him.

Starting in the garden of Eden, God has pursued a friendship relationship with us. So we know that friendships are something God highly values as productive relationships. The next chapter reveals how God-inspired friendships operate and bear good fruit.

Chapter 12

Changing From Servant to Friend

BIBLICAL FRIENDSHIPS GIVE us a picture of the intensity of relationships that God desires with us. We see this in the lives of both David and Jonathan.

The friendship between Jonathan and David was powerful. They developed the kind of bond that would cause a man to turn his back on family. The Bible describes the connection as a knitting together of souls (1 Sam. 18:1). David was so fixed in Jonathan's heart that Jonathan was willing to defy the king, his own father, Saul. There is a friendship so fixed in a person's heart that loyalty of any other nature seems common, almost empty.

Historically and scripturally it seems Jonathan was as capable of inspiring loyalty as he was bestowing it. On one occasion Jonathan was making a decision whether or not the Lord would have him single-handedly attack a garrison of Philistines. The only company he requested was his armor bearer. Without hesitation this young man responded:

> Do all that is in your mind; I am with you in
> whatever you think [best].
> —1 SAMUEL 14:7, AMP.

In the previous chapter of 1 Samuel we find the fact that makes this statement powerful: there were only two swords in all of Israel. Saul had one and Jonathan had the other. Jonathan's armorbearer hadn't any sword or spear. All he had was his master's shield. If Jonathan didn't protect him, he was a goner. He had no way of defending himself.

I can see them standing back to back and fighting. The armorbearer holds the shield high to stop any blows from behind and Jonathan fiercely protects them both from the front.

True friendship involves believing in and trusting a person to the point of a willingness to lay down your family or even your life for another.

Jesus said that no greater love has any man than that of laying down his life for another (John 15:13). He also said that if a man were not willing to abandon even his family he wasn't truly fit for the kingdom. He said that if you loved father, mother or even son or daughter more than Him you were not worthy of Him (Matt. 10:37).

I have had a few friendships that were at least bordering on these levels. These are people so close to me that we are able to lay aside the protective walls with which we naturally surround ourselves. Laying these aside provides new opportunities for spiritual growth by creating opportunities to speak into one another's lives.

For true friendship there must be this kind of openness. It creates the opportunity to speak encouragement and strength along with correction. The spirit of offense cannot exist in this environment. Personal opinions and suggestions are not just tolerated but respected and prayerfully considered.

A few years ago I was introduced to a young man who was just beginning to itinerate. I had never heard him even on tape. Although he had already written a couple of books, I hadn't had an opportunity to read them. But when he was recommended to me I felt a quickening in my spirit that he was to come to DayStar.

On the Sunday morning he was to begin the meetings we had a blow-out worship service. People were rejoicing and worshipping. Some were weeping. During the song service sinners were drawn to the altar without an altar call and were saved. It was incredible. I finally went to the platform and introduced our guest.

He rose quickly from his seat, went to the pulpit and with fire in his eyes said: "The Lord says, 'I smell religion in this place and it stinks!'"

The whole church went dead silent. I began to pray to myself and ask the Lord if I hadn't made a terrible mistake in inviting this man, and yet I didn't feel any quenching of the Spirit. The Holy Spirit spoke to my heart and said, "This is Me! Leave it alone." I did. And out of this man came a word from the Lord that was so true and specific that only the Holy Spirit could have known. I knew immediately that this man feared God much more than man, and I set my mind to make him my friend.

His name is John Bevere. We are friends. He has

the right to speak into my life at any and all times. I may not like what he says, but I never get angry with him. And I have that right to speak to him. And I will never abuse it because I know his heart.

I have just two or three friends like that. It takes many years to find the kind of person where your hearts knit. But once you make this kind of friend, time and distance are never a factor.

I have another friend named Nevile McDonald who pastors in South Africa. We are friends. Even if we are in our own countries and haven't communicated in months, we both know if we are needed we will get the call. And the person who is calling knows the other will take the call and do whatever is humanly possible to help.

Though these peer friendships are strong, the very closest friends I have are my wife and children. Both of my sons are in ministry, and I know they know me, good and bad, at my best and at my worst. And yet they still love and respect me. Certainly no one on earth knows me better than my own wife. But Jesus is beyond that. I know that He knows me better than I know myself, and yet He has accepted me. I believe He is always going to do what is best for me. No matter what. I trust Him implicitly. And by His acceptance, I know I am His friend.

CULTIVATING FRIENDSHIP WITH JESUS

Friendships don't just happen. They must be worked on and cultivated. You may reach a place where you know each other, but it isn't ever by accident. Paul said of knowing God:

[For my determined purpose is] that I may
know Him [that I may progressively become
more deeply and intimately acquainted with
Him, perceiving and recognizing and understanding the wonders of His Person more
strongly and more clearly], and that I may in
that same way come to know the power out-
flowing from His resurrection [which it
exerts over believers], and that I may so
share His sufferings as to be continually
transformed [in spirit into His likeliness
even] to His death, [in the hope].
—PHILIPPIANS 3:10, AMP.

I want to know Him like that! The Greek verb for
knowing is the same one used when the Bible said
Mary knew not a man (Luke 1:34). It means intimacy
almost to a sexual knowledge. I live my life to know
Him. It takes patience and long hours of prayer and
mediation on the Word. I haven't arrived yet, but I
slip in and out on occasion. I want to get in and stay
in. I don't know if that's possible for me, but I know
it's possible according to the Word.

The Bible speaks prophetically about having a
friendship relationship with God when it states that
"there is a friend that sticketh closer than a brother"
(Prov. 18:24, KJV).

Let me give an illustration of this. We find two disciples betraying Jesus in the last hours of His life.
They are Judas and Simon Peter. But their reactions
to the results of their betrayal are diametrically
opposed.

When Judas sees that Jesus is crucified, he is filled
with remorse. Not only does everyone know his role

in Jesus' arrest, but the end result doesn't justify his action by any stretch of the imagination. Being embarrassed, ashamed and possessing no hope of being restored, he goes out and hangs himself (Matt. 27:5).

Simon Peter, on the other hand, weeps bitterly (Matt. 26:75) after realizing his verbal betrayal but ultimately comes back into relationship with Jesus (Matt. 26:75).

There are many similarities between Judas and Simon Peter. Both men were advised by Jesus that He already knew their hearts. Both men thought they knew better than Jesus what would or should transpire. Both were embarrassed by the results of their actions. But Simon Peter seemed to know Jesus better than Judas even though both disciples had spent approximately the same amount of time following Him. Judas' response is hopelessness resulting in suicide. Simon's response is helplessness that results in surrender.

I personally believe that it is through this very experience and the interview that follows on the beach (John 21:15–18) that Simon draws so close to Jesus that later it seems as though their very shadows mix.

A FRIEND WHO PROTECTS

Jesus is the kind of friend who sticks closer than a brother. He is a protector. His word will be true to us at all times in every situation. Jesus is the Word made flesh (John 1:14). Even when relatives would turn against us or harm us, Jesus stays true. In fact, Paul told Timothy, "If we are faithless [do not believe and are untrue to Him], He remains true (faithful to His

Word and His righteous character), for He cannot deny Himself" (2 Tim. 2:13, Amp.).

Let me give you an illustration from the Old Testament of this powerful principle.

> You are my hiding place and my shield; I hope in Your word.
> —PSALM 119:114, AMP.

Oral tradition says that this Psalm speaks of an incident recorded in 2 Kings 11. Ahaziah the king of Judah died, and his mother Athaliah was so used to running the kingdom through her son that she usurped the throne. She had all of her grandchildren killed. But her daughter Jehosheba was married to the high priest of Jehovah. Jehosheba grabbed Joash, the youngest son of the king, and stole him before he could be killed. She took him to her husband Jehoiada, and at first he hid the child in a closet where extra bedding was kept. But this became dangerous because a decree went forth saying that if anyone had any of the king's children they would be killed. Jehoiada couldn't even trust the other priests. But he had a promise to stand on. The Lord had sworn to David that there would always be a seed from his lineage. So Jehoiada knew that since Joash was the last of the seed of David that Jehovah would protect him.

After a short time he had to move this infant son of the king. So he took him to a place above the Holy of Holies in the temple. There was a builder's scaffolding there from erecting the walls.

This hiding place worked beautifully. Whenever there was a noise the priests thought it was God in the Holy of Holies. Once when the sunlight coming from the upper windows hit Joash, his shadow fell across the Holy of Holies, but the priests thought it was just God. He was hidden there for six years until the kingdom was restored to him.

The story of Joash is an example of God as friend and protector. God made a promise to David, which is why He protected Joash generations later. As I get close to Jesus I find it nearly impossible to hurt any of His family, even if it would be to my benefit. But He is that way toward me also. As I draw closer I never have to protect myself. When God defends Himself it always overflows to cover me also.

When I got saved, my father was not a Christian. When the Lord sent me to Bible college to prepare for ministry, I worried about my dad. But I knew Jesus would take care of the situation. A year later my dad got saved at the church where I had gotten saved. Not only that—he also received a call to preach. In fact, before my dad died I had the privilege of ordaining him into the ministry. My dad became a pastor!

Why? Because Jesus is my friend, He took care of my dad. As David was a friend to Saul for Jonathan, Jesus was a friend to my dad for me.

I don't begin to pretend to have all the answers. In fact, I don't even have all of the questions. But this I know: When everything gets to bare bone and nothing seems to work, three things remain constant:

1. Jesus loves me; the Bible says so.
2. I love Jesus; He knows my heart, and it doesn't matter whether anyone else knows my heart or not.
3. Everything else is subject to change.

If I don't understand how or why in any given situation, I will wait on Him and He will tell me because He tells His friends everything. If I'm not hearing then I need to take a good look at my relationship with Him. Something is missing. My relationship has probably slacked. It is time again to lay down life and ministry and spend time getting to know my Friend.

The closer-than-a-brother relationship can be personally expensive. Many people are looking for million-dollar answers to two-bit prayers, prayed out of a ten-cent relationship. They are bargain hunters wanting Tiffany jewelry at Wal-Mart prices.

Let me give you an example. King Amaziah was about to go to war with Edom. He hired one hundred thousand mercenaries from the tribe of Ephraim for one hundred talents of silver. Unfortunately, the men from Ephraim were Baal worshippers.

A prophet came and warned him about using the devil's crowd to fight the devil (2 Chron. 25:5–9). The reply of Amaziah was, "What about the money?" The cost was uppermost in his mind—as though the God who would bring defeat over Edom might not be good for one hundred talents.

Your question might be also, "What will it cost to be a friend of Jesus?"

The answer is "everything." It will cost your life and all it contains. It will cost your fear, your emptiness, your brokenness, your ambitions, your goals. It will take it all. But the return is far more than you will ever give up. He will become your friend.

Chapter 13

True Friendship

OUR FLESH DESIRES pampering. We want to surround ourselves with people who give us what we want whenever we want. But those kinds of friendships keep us from growing. If we aren't careful we can become spoiled and petulant.

True friendships have many facets. The greatest facet must be genuine love. This love is more interested in our welfare than our pleasure. It seeks our personal growth more than our personal ease. A true friend is more interested in us than even the return they might receive from our relationship. This chapter defines true friendship and tells how to choose friends who will draw us closer to God. If we don't learn how to value and identify good, solid and true friendships we will never be able to move into or prize the friend-relationship with Jesus.

As we begin to understand this kind of friendship,

our attitudes concerning who is or is not a friend may change drastically. We may find that our truest friend may not be the person who gets us what we want. But in actuality our best friend is that person who does what we need for mental, physical or spiritual growth. Let me give you an example out of Jesus' most trying hour.

MY FRIEND JUDAS

Jesus was about to be betrayed by the stinging kiss of one of His closest associates. As He saw this betrayer coming, backed by a consort of soldiers, Jesus said something so startling that at first I thought it must be sarcasm. Judas strolled up to Jesus as though nothing were wrong, and Jesus said, "Friend, for what are you here?" (Matt. 26:50, Amp.).

We know Jesus never lied. Not one word of Scripture is untrue. Yet Jesus had already stated that Judas was a thief (John 12:6) and that he was a devil (John 6:70–71). We might ask, then, how could Jesus possibly see him as a friend?

Jesus had stated that His meat—his very substance—was to do the will and pleasure of His father and to completely finish His work (John 4:34). He knew He couldn't fulfill the mission of His Father unless Judas betrayed Him. In fact, it was the only way He could join His Father in heaven and still fulfill prophecy. It also was the only way to make provision for those He loved.

Jesus was saying, in essence, anyone who helps Him fulfill the Father's will and finish His work is a friend.

On the other hand, when Simon Peter tried to get in the way of Jesus going to Jerusalem and being crucified, Jesus immediately called him Satan and told him to get out of the way (Matt. 16:22-23).

These two scenarios lead us to draw two conclusions: 1) a true friend is one who is helping us get closer to the person and will of Jesus, even if on the surface they appear to be and feel as though they are our worst enemy and 2) anyone who tries to keep us from the will of God, even if it is by pampering and blessing us physically or emotionally, has become a devilish enemy.

SELECTING FRIENDS

I believe that everything in Christianity rises and falls on relationships. We had to get a relationship with Jesus to even get in to God's kingdom. Even on a human level we must surround ourselves with people wrapped up in Jesus (if these principles hold water.) We are making choices every day as to what we really wish to become in Jesus.

There isn't any way for me to fully convey the importance of choosing friends wisely. The old saying "Birds of a feather flock together" is full of spiritual truth. If any of us wants a quick survey of our own spiritual depth, all we really have to do is examine the friends closest to us. But we need to brace ourselves for the shock that may follow.

We also need to look at the kind of leaders we are attracted to. Do we want them to challenge us from God's Word? Or do we want them to make us feel good? The people of Israel had a true friend to lead them out of Egypt, but those who were immature followed a leader who just wanted to make them happy.

Moses loved the people of Israel, but they did tend

to get on his nerves. As he moved into the leadership role to which God had called him, he firmly called upon Pharaoh to "let My people go" (Ex. 5:1, Amp.). By the time we get to Exodus 32:11 Moses was saying, "Why does Your wrath blaze hot against Your people?" (Amp.) And then when we get to verse 31 of the same chapter Moses referred to Israel as "this people." The implication seems to be that neither Moses nor the Lord really wants to claim them.

Nevertheless, Moses prayed, "Yet now, if You will forgive their sin—and if not, blot me, I pray You, out of Your book which You have written!" (Ex. 32:32, Amp.) In nearly every translation there is a dash after the word sin. I believe this is where Moses stopped to weep and intercede. It is an expression of a man choked by tears as he is overwhelmed by both weariness and love. Moses was exasperated by the people's actions, but he loved them enough to intercede in their behalves and correct or rebuke them when that would be best for them. He was such a friend to Israel that when he died the Bible says Israel wept for him in the plains of Moab for thirty days (Deut. 34:8).

We can learn something about the character of Moses by comparing the mourning for his death and the mourning for Aaron's death. Scripture says "Israel" mourned Moses. Upon examination of the Hebrew we find out that the word translated *Israel* traditionally speaks specifically of the mature Jewish males. It is the word *Yisrael*. The mature were going to miss Moses' leadership. They knew they needed a leader who loved them enough to correct them.

On the other hand, when Aaron died the Bible speaks of the "congregation" mourning (Num. 20:29). This Hebrew word for *congregation* is *edah*, which is feminine. In this context it traditionally speaks of those who are weaker or less mature. The context then gives the sense that the immature and faint of heart mourned Aaron, who was quicker to give in to their desires and sensual demands, more than they mourned Moses.

The immature often fail to appreciate the friendship of one who loves them enough to guide them into what is best. But the mature want a friend who will tell them the truth, even when it hurts.

AVOIDING ERROR

In the epistles we find several references to leaders who gain popularity by satisfying "itching ears" (2 Tim. 4:3, Amp.).

Paul wrote to the church at Thessalonica:

> For as you well know, we never resorted either to words of flattery or to any cloak to conceal greedy motives or pretexts for gain, [as] God is our witness. Nor did we seek to extract praise *and* honor *and* glory from men, either from you or from anyone else, though we might have . . .
> —1 THESSALONIANS 2:5–6, AMP.

Paul then continued to express that they were so loved by him that he had lead them as a father rather than a ruler. He had exhorted, stimulated, encouraged and charged them as a father to live lives worthy of God (vv. 11–12).

Simon Peter in his second epistle picked up the same theme.

> For uttering loud boasts of folly, they beguile *and* lure with lustful desires of flesh those who are barely escaping from them who are wrongdoers. They promise them liberty, when they themselves are the slaves of depravity *and* defilement—for by whatever anyone is made inferior *or* worse *or* is overcome, to that [person or thing] he is enslaved.
>
> —2 PETER 2:18–19, AMP.

Often those who are speaking the nice words that appease our senses and self-esteem are not really our friends at all. This kind of relationship often results in a person being led into error. They tell us what we want or like to hear, and we follow them into a pit. The blind leading the blind is the way Jesus put it, with the result of both leader and follower ending up in a ditch (Matt. 15:14).

I believe there are many who have backslidden over bitterness accumulated by a misunderstanding of friendship. They expected God to be a heavenly sugar daddy who would place them on a pedestal of power and authority, but instead they found a loving father who led them into difficult situations that challenged them to trust Him more.

Several years ago a young man asked me to mentor him. I was secretly very flattered, but I didn't respond out of that. Instead I said, "If you really want me to mentor you then meet me every day Monday through Friday at 5:00 A.M. in the sanctuary beginning tomorrow. We will pray together two to three hours or more each day. If you don't want to do that I really don't have time for you."

I know I shocked him, but he took the challenge. We met together for more than two years. To this very day we are great friends. I knew that a friendship that didn't challenge him would never be of benefit to him.

I want the Lord to love me so much that He is constantly making room for Himself in me. It will keep me from error. And I intend to surround myself with friends that will challenge me just to stay up with them in their relationship with the Lord.

In the final chapter of this book I want to answer one final question: How much are relationships worth in God's eyes?

Chapter 14

Making the Investment

I MENTIONED BRIEFLY that there is great cost in the type of friendship I have been describing. But the cost isn't loss. I know it may sound as if I'm suggesting you throw your life, energy and resources away on the person who is the object of your relationship. But this isn't how it is at all. A better description would be investment. Everything you put into the relationship is an investment into the future. This is why Jesus can take someone with no apparent hope for a productive future and pour Himself into him.

Look at how Jesus invested in the life of a woman named Mary. Luke says Jesus delivered her from seven demons, which makes me wonder how people knew there were seven.

Please permit me a little poetic license. I see Jesus first setting this woman free from a spirit of fear. Then the next day a disciple comes to Jesus and informs him that Mary is doing pretty good but she is still having difficulty with a seductive spirit. So Jesus calls her to Himself and deals with that one.

The next day another disciple tells Jesus that although there is definite change in Mary's life she is still struggling with an affinity with wine. So Jesus deals with that one. Then a few hours later another disciple lets Jesus know she wants to be free in another area. This goes on until seven are dealt with.

Now it matters little if this scenario covered days or hours or just minutes. The fact is that Jesus stayed with it until it was complete. Many probably would have given up. People often find it easy to give up on others who aren't progressing as fast as they think they should. But Jesus could see the potential in this woman. This is the woman who would anoint Him for burial (Matt. 26:7). She was the one person besides Jesus Himself who would be spoken of wherever the gospel is preached (v. 13).

When you see the potential in people it is easier to invest in their lives. In fact, the only thing that will really live beyond us is what we put in others. Even as a pastor, I believe I must be more interested in my staff and congregation's destiny than in how I personally can be benefited by them. I must look for the potential in them. I must actively exhort them to pursue their personal destiny in Christ. If not, then I am a hireling producing hirelings.

GOD'S INVESTMENT IN US

In my relationship with Jesus I must believe that everything He says to me by the Spirit or through the Word is His investment into my life. He truly wants better for me than I want for myself.

If I can grasp this then I realize that having faith in Him and His Word is simply an investment on my part that will always bring a great return.

For example, let's look at Luke 15—the story we all know as that of the prodigal son. I see an old man walking out to his barn to speak to his foreman. He greets his foreman and inquires as to the work schedule for the day. The foreman lays out his plans.

"I'm sending the new man out to the back forty to plow, and I've got two men who are going to work on the fences. I have a couple of guys who are going to take the sheep to the back side of the desert for fresh grass, and another man will herd the cattle into the new range."

"Is that all?" the old man asks.

"I think so," replies the foreman.

"Are you sure?" says the old man, with a little agitation creeping into his voice.

"That's all I can remember," says the foreman.

"I told you," sputters the old man. "I told you that whatever you do—no matter what else is done—you had better feed that calf. I'm not going to put up with anybody not feeding the calf."

"Yes, sir," is the quick reply. "I haven't forgotten. I am going to do that myself."

The old man walks out to his station at the end of the path to his home where he stands on a rock peering down the road. At the same time the foreman is approached by one of his workers, who inquires as to the basis of all that exchange.

The foreman relates the story of this man's youngest son, who asked for his inheritance and left town. "No one really knows if the boy is even alive.

But our master says he had a promise out of the Bible—Proverbs 22:6. It says that if you teach a child right while they are young, sooner or later they are coming back. He believes that it's like a hook in that boy's jaw that will eventually bring him home, and he has us keep a calf fatted and ready for that return. It's sort of his investment in that promise."

While they are talking they fail to notice what is happening out by the road. The old man is looking intently. There is a little agitation in his stance. He has seen something. Someone's coming. The lone figure looks a little too old and thin and ragged to be his boy. But the way he carries himself triggers something in the old man's memory. He leaps off his perch and runs and embraces his boy. That which was lost has been found, and the calf is ready.

As we understand that friendship is both a relationship of mutual love and also an investment in the future, we will begin to grasp the power of the kingdom of God.

True, biblical and godly friendship will operate in the parameters of selflessness and giving. The real friend cannot let terms like *surrender* and *submission* ever get in the way of their love. Exhortation, encouragement and correction must all carry the same value. It will cost to be a friend. But the rewards far outweigh the investment. The decision is yours. Do you know Him? Do you know Him as friend?